John Seymour Wood

Gramercy Park

A story of New York

John Seymour Wood

Gramercy Park
A story of New York

ISBN/EAN: 9783744747356

Printed in Europe, USA, Canada, Australia, Japan

Cover: Foto ©ninafisch / pixelio.de

More available books at **www.hansebooks.com**

Gramercy Park

A STORY OF NEW YORK

BY

JOHN SEYMOUR WOOD

NEW YORK
D. APPLETON AND COMPANY
1892

COPYRIGHT, 1892,
BY D. APPLETON AND COMPANY.

PRINTED AT THE
APPLETON PRESS, U. S. A.

"Separate—what comes? Fust it's like the circulation of your blood a-stoppin'—all goes wrong. Then there's misunderstandin's—ye've both lost the key. Then, behold ye, there's birds o' prey hoverin' over each on ye, an' it's which'll be snapped up fust. Then, oh dear! oh dear! it be like the devil come into the world again."

MRS. BERRY, IN RICHARD FEVEREL.

GRAMERCY PARK.

I.

JACK DE FORD wandered along the sunny side of Irving Place, northward, until he found himself presently in the maze of Gramercy Park. He was quite early, this bright May morning, and, as he was not required to be at his office before half-past nine, he had determined to take the elevated at Twenty-third, instead of Fourteenth Street, as was his wont. The high iron fence around the pretty square, and the apparent absence of any entrance or gateway, gave the solitary couple whom he saw walking within the enclosure the air of prisoners. He stood a moment gazing absently at the white, pretty fountain in the centre, which gave forth a pleasant musical sound. On either side of the fountain were beds of brilliant vari-colored tulips. There were comfortable benches along the gravel walks, and the shade-trees were already leaved in a luxuriant green. He quickly made up his mind, so charming was the prison, that he was barred out, rather than that the two people, walking at a distance within, were prisoners in the little park. He divined that the absence of gateways was but a sign of aristocratic exclusiveness. It was too early for nurse-maids and children, too early for the usual policeman. The promenaders had the place entirely to themselves. They approached, around a turn in the gravel-path, the spot where he stood looking through the bars. It appeared that a very handsome young girl was taking her constitutional on the arm of a robust, stout little old gentleman in gray side-whiskers. They walked rapidly, the young girl talking—and talking in a high key, very much out of breath, and with cheeks very much flushed.

De Ford was on his way down town, but he was willing to be late this mild May morning, if it cost him a "dock" in his salary. Within the green enclosure of the pretty park was the girl—the one girl he loved. He would wait and speak to them. As they came nearer he could overhear the girl speak in breathless tones:

"Papa—papa! not so fast," she was saying; "I cannot tell you all I want to say. He—he is a connection of the Archibalds, you know, and he———"

But they raced past and he could learn no more of what Florence Heath was saying—and saying about him, evidently; she—Florence Heath—who had told him so demurely, last evening, at Mrs. Canfield's dancing-class, that she could only be a sister to him. For a moment he meditated—how delightful it would be, if it were possible!—a brave rescue of the charming Florence, and, especially of her obdurate papa from their imprisonment. He longed to put that stolid, stout little man under a sense of obligation. He longed to recommend himself in some way—to show himself worthy of the girl on the little man's arm; for he felt assured that it was her father, whose hard heart and suspicious business nature had been the fundamental cause of Florence's forbidding him to "hope."

He had met the old gentleman at dancing-classes, at balls, at parties; Florence had introduced him when he came, dragon-like, at ridiculously early hours to carry her off, protesting and pouting, home. He admitted, however, that her Puritan father was able to preserve thereby in his daughter's face a certain sweet grace of health, and a dewy freshness of eye, which seemed to be denied to the late stayers. If there was anything that could mitigate his unbearable conduct, it was his quiet, intense love of this same daughter—which De Ford, very laudably, wished to share with him.

In the mean time, Florence and her papa had spurted around the little park, again with marvellous celerity. He fancied they would not see him, as he stood gazing between the iron pickets, in dumb admiration. How sweet she looked! Her large hat with its bright flowers, her dress of pale gray, her indescribable air of fashion—foretelling all the glories of summer. She was excited, brilliant, *spirituelle*, and dear to him as her father was repugnant.

"Confound him!" muttered De Ford, "he doesn't *begin* to know how lovely she is!"

And they were still talking of him. It was difficult for him to hide himself; he secretly longed to sink into the earth, and disappear; but on they came.

"Really, papa, you do him injustice; he is very well connected—the Albany De Fords, you know," cried Florence, her chin in the air. But the rest was silence; Florence's quick eye caught his own; he was conscious of a bow, which he returned, and of a pretty blush, which gave him enormous secret pleasure. He had been but a few months in New York, but he fancied he had been in the city long enough to select the most charming girl in it—or in the world—to whom to pay his devotions. He had met and danced three times with her at one of the Patriarchs' balls, and since that night had found it quite impossible to think of any one else. He had calmly bankrupted his finances in sending her "Jacks." He was prepared to do any foolish thing. As he saw her and her father approach the park-gate, his heart gave a leap of pleasure; something, he knew not what, told him it was to be his lucky day.

The old gentleman fumbled in one pocket after another—*his park-key was gone!* Florence had not seen it. Florence knew nothing about it. The old gentleman was getting angry. It was De Ford's opportunity.

However, De Ford may have scrimped and

saved in other ways, he dressed very well indeed; having his clothes over from London twice a year, by a mysterious tailor's man, who appeared at his office down town, and delivered him his "goods" with a truly romantic smuggler manner. His scarf was dark and in very good tone, and his hat was ever fresh and new. On this sunny May morning, he was particularly well-groomed; he had the consciousness, as he stood there—which Emerson tells us some women have—that well-fitting clothes afford, at times, a greater consolation than religion.

"I must have dropped the key somewhere," cried papa, very much annoyed; "I'll go back and look along the path for it."

He turned to go as he spoke, but he was by no means intending to leave Florence *en tête-à-tête* with that good-looking young scapegrace, De Ford—of all men—and so he added:

"You go one way, my dear, and I'll go the other; we shall soon find it."

"Can I be of any assistance?" said De Ford, lifting his hat, and pulling nervously at his long mustache; "I beg of you, let me go and get you a key somewhere——"

He was aware that his offer was somewhat

vague, but it was the best he could make under the circumstances.

"Oh, don't trouble yourself, Mr. De Ford; it is—it must be—in the park—somewhere——"

This was vague, too. But Florence, in spite of the painful dismissal of the evening before, had given De Ford a very charming smile. He fancied it was a smile of encouragement. It was, indeed, his belief that every woman's "no" meant "yes." He walked slowly along outside the fence, as she walked within it, searching for the lost key, and keeping pace with her. They soon, by this ingenious but simple device, were the entire distance of the park away from papa.

"Florence! Forgive me—but—I can't believe that what you said last night on the stairs was—final." De Ford spoke in a low voice, and Florence gave an agitated exclamation.

"*Papa will hear you!*" she cried; then she sighed and looked down.

As papa was at the moment at the other end of the square, he took her words figuratively, as he hoped she intended.

"Then he shall hear me—at once! I shall go to him—now!"

"Mr. De Ford— wait!" she said sedately.

"Come closer the fence, pray do—and—and—let me swear that you are all the world to me; I—did not take for granted what you said last night——"

Their eyes met, and all the love in the whole world then seemed to be in them.

"You know that I cannot live without you—that I have been wandering about all night—in my mind, I mean—hoping—expecting to catch sight of you—somehow, somewhere. Do, Florence, at least come up to the fence!"

"I dare not; papa is watching."

Yet Florence, in spite of the little sign at her feet, "Keep off the Grass," and in spite of all the civil city authorities, with a quick glance papa-ward, and a fluttering of the heart, advanced close—very close—to the high iron fence, and took his extended hand.

> "Stone walls do not a prison make
> Nor iron bars a cage!"

he quoted laughingly. So it's papa, is it, who is so cruel—so unkind? Ah, my darling, I knew it couldn't be you!"

He had drawn her gloved hand through the bars, and kissed it. There was no one to be seen—not a soul—in the street.

She tried to withdraw her hand, but he would not let it go.

"And if you do not love me—what do I care what becomes of me? I—I will join the army—the Salvation Army!"

"Jack!" It was the first time she had spoken his name, and he said rapturously:

"Ah! Then may I not hope?"

"Oh, it's only papa, it isn't I. He doesn't quite trust you—there! I've said it. Oh, he's looking—he's coming!" Her high color was charming just then. She hurried into the gravel path quickly, and began looking for the key. Papa, with what they felt to be a determined, angry stride, was bearing down upon them at a brisk pace. Florence stooped suddenly.

"Here it is!" she cried; "I've found it!"

"Quick! give it to me; I have a plan," De Ford called eagerly. "Quick, before he comes!"

"I—I can't; he will see me."

"Throw it!"

She gave one of those tentative, awkward girl throws, so amusing to a man, so exasperating to a woman, and the key fell a few feet within the fence.

"Go on pretending to search for it, dear,"

he whispered hoarsely; "I will get it with my stick."

Florence did as she was told. Just as the old gentleman came up, a few moments later, the key was safe in Jack's waistcoat pocket, and he was soberly giving directions to Florence where he believed the little article would be most likely to be found in the path.

"Very awkward!" exclaimed Mr. Heath, full of vexation and heat. "Here it is nearly ten o'clock! I must be going down town. Of course, there isn't a policeman in sight. I wonder where I dropped it. It is abominably provoking. I don't know what to do—how to get out!"

"Can't I be of some assistance *now?*" De Ford lifted his hat again with exaggerated civility.

"Oh—er—really—locked in—prisoners, you see!" laughed papa dismally, and trying his best to pass it off as a joke.

"I am fortunately acquainted with several people in the neighborhood who have keys, and, while I go in search of one, permit me to offer you a cigar, sir." De Ford boldly reached his hand through the fence. "And here's the morning paper, sir; I was just reading an interesting article about the 'public' necessity of raising the tariff still higher on Russian leather; let me advise you to take a seat on a bench, and wait for me."

"Ah, yes, thanks very much. I'm sure you're very kind, indeed."

The old gentleman looked a trifle surprised, but took the paper and cigar, and sauntered off to a bench.

"I shan't be long," said De Ford. He hurried away, really for the purpose of intercepting the park policeman, who was coming up the street with an apple and orange in either hand, and a gate-key, of course, in his pocket.

"Here's a dollar for you, officer, if you will kindly walk once more around the block."

"What's up?"

"Nothing; only as a favor to me—that's all;" and he crammed the crisp note into the policeman's hand. Florence, whose quick eyes discovered the stratagem, kept her father in conversation.

"Oh! he admires you so much, papa—he's heard so much about you! And you don't know how hard-working he is; but he says he hasn't your *capacity*—and he's a connection of the Archibalds, you know, and he says—it is true, papa—that when his grandfather dies——"

"Florence, I've told you a dozen times he hasn't a dollar in the world—no, nor a cent—but I must say he can be very civil. Most young men nowadays don't know how to be polite to their elders. Ahem! Yes, very interesting article on Russia-leather." And the old gentleman adjusted his spectacles on his nose and fell to reading.

"Mr. De Ford is so interested in leather," said Florence in a small half-whisper. Her father paid no attention to her; he had lit the cigar (a far better one than *he* ever afforded), and was feeling very comfortable, indeed, in the cool, delicious morning air of the park, amid the tulips.

"He says he is very lonely in New York; he has no place to go to—no house he can call his home;" and she sighed.

"Let him join a club," said the old gentleman gruffly.

"Oh, yes, but he says they drink wine in clubs;" and Florence Heath looked down to hide her guilty smile.

"Hum! hum! so they do," muttered her father; "let him join a church, then."

"But he says there are so many churches——"

"Many humbugs! Every one knows Dr. Surplice is the only real orthodox preacher in New York. Let him go there."

"He does go there now—he's *so* devout; but he says his mother died when he was but a year old, and his religious instruction has been wofully neglected. Papa, shall I ask him to come home with us?" She looked away. Where *was* Jack?

"Certainly not! The idea! This time of day!"

"But it's so kind of him to get the key for us——"

"Yes, but he's slow enough getting it, in all conscience!"

Although her back was turned, she knew Jack had appeared again.

"Oh, here he is at last!" she cried, and rose briskly. De Ford, who had been hiding around the corner, now hastened forward on a run. (He was a clever amateur actor, much admired as Romeo in the burlesque at Harvard, in the Pudding, in '84.) He presented the outward aspect of a man who has nearly run a desperate race for twenty blocks.

"Oh, no trouble at all," he cried breathlessly; "very glad to be of service;" and he swung the iron gate open with a flourish, and Florence and her papa passed out into the street. Florence gave him a sweet little glance. "Ah, *Ciel!* I am free once more," she laughed; and De Ford replied, under the very nose of papa:

"You know you never said a wickeder fib in your life!"

Papa looked mystified. The badinage of young people, nowadays!

"But isn't there such a thing in law as duress?" she laughed; "you had me under lock and key!"

Papa looked more mystified than ever; he sailed away with Florence on his arm, then turned:

"Oh! De Ford, come around some night and smoke a cigar with me; do you play bezique?"

And Jack went down town with a light heart. It *was* his lucky day.

II.

 A FORTNIGHT later and John Shermerhorn De Ford was solemnly, truly, unalterably, and for all time engaged. He borrowed some money of a friend, and bought an expensive ring at Sparcus'; a pretty thing in diamonds and rubies. They were engaged; but papa, who was a stern old Puritan New Englander, made conditions. He was obdurate; he was relentless; he drew up a long paper, which De Ford gladly signed. Poor fool! he was happy enough to sign a promissory note! The conditions were many. The engagement was not to be announced; there was always to be a "discreet" third person in the room. He might call Monday, and Thursdays from 8 to 10 P.M. Florence could only wear the ring in private. Papa reserved the right to break the affair sharp off at any time. Papa reserved a great many other things; they must not call each other by their first names; if they went to parties

they could only dance twice together, etc., etc.

They each signed the formal "terms" of the engagement, and secretly swore to be true, even if papa should put the world between them. Ah, there never were before or since such lovers as these!

Mrs. Heath was a mild, sweet-natured little woman, of highest family connections, who was completely under her husband's—and every one else's—thumb. She signified her "discreetness" by regularly going to sleep on Monday and Thursday evenings, when De Ford, with his usual bunch of jack-roses, called upon his *fiancée* in rigid accordance with the "terms." It may be said that, at those times, some of papa's rules were undoubtedly infringed; but, when he happened in, Jack was always reading aloud, in a solemn, dreary tone of voice, that dullest of all dull tales, "Hilliard's History of the United States." Papa began to believe that he had made a most desirable choice of a son-in-law.

Meanwhile De Ford worked very hard down-town, in the large banking and brokers' office he was in, on Wall Street. He added columns of uninteresting figures, ran with messages over to the Stock Exchange, and made himself generally useful in talking to customers over the "tape." No one can ever know, or begin to know, of the life dramas of these myriad pale, hard-worked, well-dressed, sad young men on Wall Street. De Ford had gone through his four years at Harvard sublimely indifferent to what his circumstances were to be afterward. He had belonged to the Banjo Club, the Varsity Nine, the "Dicky," and the Pudding, and that was enough. Just a year after he had left college, and was in Paris—he had been at the opera with some friends, one night—he received a telegram from his father to return home at once. When he arrived at New York, he found that he would be obliged to work for a living, that his father's fortune had melted away. Shortly after, his father died, overwhelmed by his disastrous failure. Poor Jack, as unfit for battling with fate and earning his own living as the pleasant, easy, social life of a great university could make him, came down to Wall Street very blue and miserable to begin work. As time went on, however, he got over the feeling. His naturally light and buoyant nature asserted itself. He went a little into society. He met the pretty Miss Heath—there were many *contretemps;* and now, as we have seen, he was "conditionally" engaged.

He had a bright, quick mind, and he "took" very well in Branscomb, Beach, & Catherly's. The patrons of the firm conceived a fancy for "young De Ford." "He had most admirable manners." They said: "Poor chap—he had been brought up like a prince!" They rather petted him, took him out to expensive lunches at Del's and Saverin's, where he amused them with his capital stories; they gave him fine cigars, asked his advice about "C. K., and K. C.," and other mysterious western railways, and urged him to set up an office for himself. He felt himself constantly touching millions, and in debt to his landlady at his boarding-house. It was a most peculiar life he began to lead: a life of unsubstantial brilliancy,—dining with some rich friends at Delmonico's, sending the charming Florence a box of roses, and, next day, walking up and down town to save car-fare, or bargaining with his landlady to let his bill run over a week longer. His mind was full of gorgeous visions of enormous wealth, and his happiest moments with Florence were spent in planning a rational outlay of their expected ten thousand a year.

But at last, after a time, his prospects actually began to change for the better. Branscomb died—went off in a sudden apoplexy one day, on the floor of the Stock Exchange, and there was a change in the firm. Every one in the office moved up a peg; the firm became, "Beach, Catherly, & De Ford." In honor of the event, Florence was allowed to give a dinner and theatre-party, at which their engagement was announced. Catherly, a fat, good-natured millionaire, swore that his junior should be married at once, and made it a personal matter to see papa and talk him over. Mr. Heath was obstinate, however.

"Wait," he said, cautiously, "you Wall Street men have many ups and downs; it isn't a legitimate business; it isn't leather; it isn't even coffee or flour or sugar. It's betting and gambling—that's what it is; if you bet right, you win, that's all. My future son-in-law is a gentleman—I don't say he isn't; but he and Florry are both young; they can wait a year or two. See how kind I am! I have removed several conditions;

De Ford can now call on either of the following nights, to wit (and he took out a small memorandum-book): in addition to Mondays and Thursdays, he may now call Wednesdays and Fridays; he may also come to Sunday-night tea; he may see Florry on Mondays, alone—a great concession, Mr. Catherly—for it means, Mr. Catherly, as you and I know, for we are both married men, and went through, I dare say, the experiences of courtship—it means, I fear, a respectful kiss."

"Why, of course it does!" roared jolly old Catherly. "Why shouldn't they? A handsome young chap, and the sweetest girl in the world! By heaven, sir, she's exquisite—she's a beauty!"

"But—it's all very well—but——"

"I don't want to hear of any 'buts' and concessions; I want you to let them get married; we shall see that De Ford will have five thousand a year; he's worth it; he's a valuable man; he makes friends easily; he brings them into the office——"

"I wish he was in leather," grumbled the crusty old merchant thoughtfully. "It is so much steadier."

"Well, he *isn't;* he's going to be a wealthy

banker; he's going to be a man you'll be proud to call your son-in-law!" And Catherly, with the utmost good-nature, talked at the old gentleman so cleverly and so well that he got him to say they should be married a year from that day—" conditionally."

III.

A YEAR from that day rolled quickly round. It was again one of those bright, sunny mornings in May. The tulips were out once more in Gramercy Park. It was now two years since De Ford had so gallantly rescued his lovely *fiancée* and her father from their dire imprisonment. The pretty little enclosure, with its high iron fence—the brightest spot in all the great dull New York—seemed to gleam with unusual lustre. It was high noon; there were sounds of wedding-bells in the air, coming high and clear from the city spires of old St. George's; there was happiness and jollity in all the faces one saw; the park policeman had donned new white gloves, and wore a white favor; there was an awning stretching out to the curb from the wide, old-fashioned brown-stone house of Mr. Heath. There were crowds of children and nurses, and street-gamins; and, best of all, there was poor

old Mrs. Jones, whom Florence had time to be so kind to, and old Mrs. Murphy from her "district," too, all standing there in the sunshine, looking for the bride to return from church.

Presently the carriages. The children gave a shout. The first drove up to the curb.

"Be careful, Jack—my train!" and out stepped De Ford, hale and handsome; and see how tenderly he helped his young wife alight! Then—oh, dreadful fate of these two young people—out stepped papa! For some reason papa looked unhappy and disturbed. He hurried up after the bride and groom, and then the carriages, one after the other, deposited the guests for the wedding-breakfast.

There was Catherly, resplendent in his English morning-suit, and Beach, the head of the firm, with a gorgeous button-hole bouquet; there were loads of pretty girls, for Florence was extremely popular; crowds of Jack's Harvard classmates, for he was fond of his friends; and the music from out the open windows made the park policeman "guess as they'd be dancin'."

But papa looked on askance! He was now

a father-in-law; true, but did his prerogatives cease from this day? Must he, forsooth, now hand over his sceptre? Mind you, it was his only daughter—his only child whom he had just given away "conditionally;" and he loved her as the apple of his eye! Yes, "conditionally!" He had understood that Jack would come, after a *reasonable* wedding-journey, and live with them on Gramercy Park with his wife; it was understood, but not agreed, for no words had passed.

But now Jack—his son-in-law, had put his foot down. It came like a thunder-bolt! Mr. and Mrs. De Ford intended to live in an apartment paid for out of Jack's own income; they had actually picked it out—up-town, on the West side!

Papa realized that this was simply flat rebellion, and something must needs be done about it at once. There was the great broad house on Gramercy Park, with its bay-windows, its comfortable old-fashioned belongings, which would simply be empty without Florence and her friends. Why, he would never have *thought* of giving his consent had the idea entered his head that his daughter —his only daughter—meditated such unfilial conduct. Go away from the family roof-tree, and live alone with her husband? Preposterous—ridiculous! He would put *his* foot down, too.

After the elaborate wedding-breakfast there came a crowded reception; and when the bride, in her dainty gray travelling-dress and little hat trimmed with flowers, went out the door on Jack's arm the old shoes and showers of rice, and "God bless you's," and hurrahs, were enough to set the whole park agog. "Ah, God bliss her!" cried old Mrs. Murphy. "The prettiest bride the sun ever shone on—so she is! God bliss her, fer she's twict as good as she's purty—so she is!"

IV.

THEY were not obliged to actually engage their apartment until the fall, and they made up their minds to spend the summer at some quiet little place in close proximity to 10 o'clock at Wall Street. They would begin their married life, *not* in conformity with the general rule for the summer months which prevailed among most of their friends, *i. e.*, a limited divorce—*they* would never be separated; and, indeed, they all spent a very pleasant summer together in a cottage at Sea Bright, and papa was as mild and reasonable as possible; for, so far, all went as papa wished.

But, unfortunately, late September came, and September fogs, and with them the necessity of coming back to town.

His father-in-law was a man of resources, and, for that matter, so was De Ford. Each had quietly gone about his plans. Papa secretly redecorated the interior of the Gramercy Park house in most sumptuous style. The third floor was hung in satin and tapestry and embossed in stamped leather from his own tanneries. Florry's sitting-room was made a charming, fascinating chamber, all in ivory white, with an exquisite old fauteuil in imitation of one in an old French chateau, and in yellow tiles from Holland. The windows were changed into little diamond-paned casements, and looked out on the greenery of the pretty park as from some lordly castle upon its demesne. There were rugs from Samarcand and furniture from Gerter's. He gave his decorator *carte blanche*. Poor man, he was not the first to be captured by a decorator! The whole house was changed into the most artistic and delightful interior. He spent a fortune on his oak dining-room, with tall gothic chairs from old Provence. Jack, on the other hand, made secret visits to the twelve-storied apartment, the "Senegambia," on upper Broadway and Central Park. He met Florence, as it were, by stealth, and they had the most delightful days in town together in hot August (when nobody but poor lonely club and business men remained in New York), purchasing cheap furniture on Fourteenth

Street. In a week or two the little flat was furnished from parlor to kitchen; brand new beds, brand new chairs, new carpets, new brooms, new frying-pans. What fun it was to cheapen flat-irons, and get ice picks at a reduction too, because they took a dozen of them! If papa went up to town by boat they went by rail, and *vice versa*. He never found them out. They were too busy to discover what he was about. They bought a most remarkable dinner-set, and decorated their parlor with the pictures Jack had in his rooms at Harvard; and when everything was done and all was ready, they said: "Of course when papa sees how lovely it is, he will yield."

And papa, at Gramercy Park, surveying his (decorator's) superb exhibition of art and taste, said:

"Oh, of course there will be no trouble about it when they see what I have done for them."

And so the eventful day came at last when they moved back to town.

V.

HIS father-in-law was even willing to make great concessions. He had pondered the matter long, and he was even prepared, *de minimis non curat,* to yield the head of the table. They came up to town by the Long Branch boat—that last day of their vacation—and, as they sat out on deck, and the goddess of Liberty hove in sight on the port bow, he said, after a little cough, and laying down his morning paper:

"Jack, I feel I am getting old——"

"Oh, not at all, sir—not at all," said De Ford quickly.

"Y-a-as—I'm getting old. I've seen my best days, Jack; I want you to sit at the head of the table——"

Florence was breathless with agitation; was Jack going to be "firm" *now*, or what? Would there be a scene?

"I will not permit it sir," said Jack; then he added, "There shall be two tables—yours and mine."

"Oh, no—we shall live together; but *you* must carve."

De Ford's face grew pale with decision:

"Father—we—I——" But Florence, sitting behind her papa, gave a gesture, and he paused.

"Women are so indirect!" he thought vexedly. She got him away by himself.

"Oh, not yet, Jack dear—wait—let us go home *at first*—then we can break it to them gently—after a day or two—Jack——" She hesitated a moment; then began again, "Dear, *home* means so much to them! It is everything. Somehow, Jack, even the Senegambia doesn't seem like *home*. There are people playing a piano overhead, and there is a lady who sings just beneath. It's very pretty and nice—but it's like being in some public building——"

"But isn't it home where *I* am?"

"Yes—but——"

"But what? How are homes ever made? A man and wife should be pioneers—should begin life alone, together on their own plantation."

"But the Senegambia isn't even a plantation—it seems like a great hotel."

Then she added, after a little pause:

"It isn't—quite—home!"

And his wife pleaded so sweetly, that De Ford merely muttered, "Oh, hang it!" and then smiled.

Now the old lady, though a very quiet and oft-times sleepy old lady, was the dearest old lady in the world—and no fool. De Ford led Florence away to the bow of the boat, to talk the affair over, and mamma leaned over her husband.

"Mr. Heath—James!"

"Well, Matilda, what is it?"

Mrs. Heath looked very wise. "I know their secret."

Papa began to have delightful visions. He turned a cheerful lobster red in consequence.

"No—not *that*——"

"Well, what is it?"

"They have taken a flat—and they've furnished it!"

Papa rose to his feet, astounded.

"No, I'll not believe it of them! That would be—*treason!*" He could think of no other more appropriate term.

"They have, and I know where it is—in the Senegambia. I found a bill of their furniture!"

"Well—well—well!" said the old gentleman unsteadily; "can it be possible? Florry leave her home? I'll not believe it—and *I'll not have it!*" He struck his fist heavily on the handrail of the steamer.

"James, you *must!* I was born in the old house in Second Avenue, and you took me away, James—yes, you did."

"But there were three of you—Florry is our only one. I've set my heart on her living in the old house on the Park; and when the children come, Matilda, and we grow old, we can sit and watch them at play from our window."

He fairly trembled with disappointment; his wife was all excitement too. To these two old people, their daughter was ever a young child.

"I have a plan," said mamma; "they *shall* live in the old house, and you shall see." But as Jack returned with Florence just then, her voice sank into a whisper which papa alone could hear.

VI.

DE FORD agreed with his wife to postpone actually going to the Senegambia until the next day. He went to his office from the boat, and as the market was exceedingly active—it generally is in September, when the brokers are only too anxious to be in the country—the smart office-boy had some reason for hoisting above his desk in the outer office the placard,

"THIS IS OUR BUSY DAY!"

De Ford was kept very late over his books, and did not arrive at the old house in Gramercy Park until six o'clock. He took the elevated train at Hanover Square, and came up town, crushed and jammed amid a band of Italian brigands and German peasants, and holding on for dear life to the strap. When he arrived at Twenty-third Street, he was in no very enviable frame of mind. He wished he had decided the matter in the morning, and had it over with. He wished, too, that

Florry had more decision of character. Of course it was best for them to live independently in their own apartment, with their own things around them. De Ford had a great fund of honest pride, and he did not want to have it said on Wall Street that he was living, as the saying is, "on the old man." During the summer he had seen more of his father-in-law than ever before; and, to tell the truth, he admitted to himself that the old gentleman was at heart a good fellow. It began to dawn on the clever young man that the intensest love of their daughter animated almost everything that the old couple said and did. Jack and his father-in-law often sat out late, while the moon danced over the sea, and every one else had gone in, smoking and talking of Florry. They both loved the sweet young girl-wife, and they could talk over what she said and did without a jealous pang. She was blithe, gay, impulsive, charming. Papa told of what she said as a two-year-old; of her running away when only three, escaping out of the open front-door, carelessly left ajar, and how after hours of the most terrible anxiety, she was brought back to the old house, chattering and laughing in the arms of a Park policeman. De Ford thought of this as he mounted the steps and groped for the usual door-bell. He was rather surprised to note the new and elaborate oaken door, and the half-windows of rich stained glass. He pressed the button and the servant opened the door, and ushered him into a most gorgeous hallway. It certainly was *not* his father-in-law's.

"I—I must have made a mistake in the number; is this—is this Mr. Heath's?" He believed he had gone up the wrong high stoop. "No, this is Mr. De Ford's, sir," and the man, dressed in subdued livery, bowed respectfully. He did not catch the name distinctly, and turned to go. Just then he heard ringing laughter, and his wife came running out of the reception room; she threw herself into his arms tumultuously and kissed him.

"It is all a surprise—and papa has done it all for us—from garret to cellar—it has all been done by Gerter—and now" (she became suddenly serious) "*we must leave it all.*"

"Yes," he said. She looked down and her face fell.

"And Jack—O Jack! you should see the

dearest little sitting-room for me upstairs—and everything!"

It only made De Ford the more determined. The very lavishness of the display of wealth on either hand affected him disagreeably. *He* hadn't paid for it. He hadn't any right to live in it. His father's failure and his struggle for independence had eaten its way into his character, and made him rather hard and insistent upon certain things. He resolved to take his wife away at once; he wished she did not have a cent in the world.

"Come, Florry, let us go now — immediately, before we have to have a scene; I am tired—I don't feel like a row just now. Let's go off to the 'Senegambia', and leave a note for them. Come, dear, let us slip away; it's all very kind, no doubt, to do all this for us; and, I must say, the old house looks like a palace; but we must not yield—we've talked the matter over again and again, and every time come to the same conclusion; we've bought our furniture; everything is awaiting us——"

"But Jack, dear, the china is all Sèvres," she whimpered.

"I don't care if it's gold."

"But the dinner is waiting—papa and mamma are both out. Wait till they come in, dear, won't you? Don't let us be rude." Florence was fluttering about like some wild wood bird caught in his hand, and held against her will.

"No, darling." He gave her a determined look, and she wilted beneath it and grew docile. But presently she fell to crying on his shoulder.

"Jack—Jack," she said, "they *love* me so!"

Poor De Ford was touched; there *was* another aspect of the case which, indeed, was rather pathetic. The old house, with its modern luxury and grandeur, would be empty and dull enough now without its brightest jewel. The exquisite young bride was more fitted to Gramercy Park than to the modest flat in the Senegambia. Had he, after all, the right to take the jewel out of its setting? But he put these ideas far from him as "sentimental."

"Come, Florry, let us hasten—think what jolly fun it will be—(by Jove! what a magnificent portière!) Get your hat, dearest; and remember, if we make a stand *now* it will make us feel so much more—er—more —well, *noble*; we shall be independent."

"But I don't want to be independent of—mamma."

However, in a moment more Florence, tearful, yet appreciating the highly creditable instinct of her husband, clung to his arm, and they were quickly on their way to their own little home. She felt that what they were doing was splendidly heroic.

"After all," whispered Jack, "it's only giving up the 'unearned increment!'"

"What's that, Jack?" she asked innocently; but he only kissed her, and they closed the fine glass door tragically behind them.

VII.

IT *was* heroic, and, too, it was such fun! It was an escapade, an elopement. They stopped and had a little dinner at a famous restaurant to emphasize it, before going on to the Senegambia. Jack was so jolly! Florence dried her tears in very dry champagne, and drowned her filial repentance in Jack's proud sense of honor. If she felt guilty—it was just enough to add a spice and tinge the affair with interest. Thoughts of poor papa and mamma coming home and expecting to find them admiring the new interior, and only pleading to be allowed to remain there always—did occasionally flit across her mind; she knew it was very, very unkind. But, then, going up in the hansom about the southwest corner of Fortieth Street, on the avenue, just past the dull lamp-post, Jack took her in his arms and kissed her—and she—she forgot it!

The Senegambia rose like an enormous

tower full twelve stories into the air, fronting on upper Broadway. The entrance was very ornate and elegant, with a variety of stained glass, and polished granite. The hallway was brilliant with electric lights. The door stood open, and the elevator-boy leaned wearily against the side of the car as they entered and requested to be lifted to the tenth story.

"They's two folks gone up there already," said the boy drowsily.

"Why, who can they be?" queried Florence.

"Old lady and old gent. 'Tween you 'n' me, mum, they seemed to want to keep it on the dead quiet, too."

"Why, it can't be papa?" she glanced at her husband.

The elevator rose to the floor, and they got out. They softly let themselves in their flat. Here and there in the cosey little parlor were pieces of new furniture done up in gunny cloth. They heard voices in the dining-room, and tiptoed out along the narrow hallway, and hid behind the door, peeping in. There was papa, his coat off, bustling about, and making a salad; and there was mamma, her skirt pinned up to her waist, running in and out of the snug little kitchen, laughing and going on like a young girl. She was broiling a steak herself and making coffee. They seemed as happy as two children, and—what? Papa actually caught hold of mamma, and gave her a hearty kiss on her ruddy cheek. They were a picture of a modern Darby and Joan.

"Oh, it is *so* like old times!" said mamma, thinking of her girlhood when Mr. Heath and she first set up housekeeping. "And if they do not want us, James, then why should we keep the great old house, now so grand and fine, for us old folk?"

"Old folk! I like that!" cried papa, "I feel as young as—as——"

Papa could think of no adequate simile, but finally admitted that it was a daisy, or perhaps a sunflower of some kind.

"And when they find that we have stolen a march on them, and that we mean to give *them* the old house on Gramercy Park for *them alone*—and that we won't live there, and we won't go there often—except once in a while—James, I must—I *must* see Florry once a week—then how glad they'll be!"

"Yes, how glad they'll be," echoed papa, rather dolefully. "The old house is too big for us—entirely. We don't need so much room; *they* do—they must entertain. I want Jack, as he grows older, to be the biggest magnate on Wall Street, and he *will* be in time. Oh, how pleased they will be when they see all I've done for them, and how I've fixed up the old place and all; and, Matilda, Jack's right—quite right. It's better to live alone—we like it, don't we? only—only! But there! now your steak is burning!"

Mamma gave a cry and ran out into the kitchen, and then soon reappeared, laughing, with the steak and coffee, and Darby and Joan sat down to their dinner. They talked of the old days, so long ago in Second Avenue; they talked of Florence—of her sweet babyhood and childhood; they spoke of their son who died—that Jack had taken his place. They seemed to think only of their children —their *two* children.

Florence stood leaning against the doorway; she was perfectly motionless, only the tears rolled down one by one. Jack had hold of her soft, warm hand.

"Come, dear," he whispered, fearing she was about to speak; "leave them alone, bless them! They are so happy—*and papa has won!*"

She gave him a quick, bright glance.

"Oh, there is but one thing—now—to be done," he whispered and nodded.

On their way out he gave the elevator-boy a dollar bill not to speak of their going there.

"It's all right, is it?" asked the boy; "he said as he was your father, so I let him up. Well, I'm queered if them tenth-floor-east-flat folks ain't a mighty bad lot—counterfeiters, *sure!*" he muttered, and afterward confided the same to the engineer, who occasionally emerged from the subterranean cellars of the Senegambia, as far as his head and shoulders went, and passed the time of day.

On their way back to Gramercy Park they stopped at a telegraph-office, and sent a messenger-boy back to the Senegambia with one of Jack's visiting-cards, on which he had scribbled a few words, which gave the old people endless amusement and delight. It obviated all further explanations, and resulted in four very happy people sitting down to a late supper that night in the old home, at which Jack, under protest, did the honors at the head of the table.

Here is the card:

Mr. & Mrs. John Schermerhorn De Ford,

At Home,

Every Day in the Week
FOREVER!   *No. — Gramercy Park.*

VIII.

THE THIRD winter came and went in Gramercy Park — a winter of quiet domestic happiness, of gentle family-life.

May came again, and the crocuses, tulips and the budding trees, and brought another little baby-life into the old house, but left the sweet young mother for days at death's door.

One night Florence lay very low. She scarcely seemed to breathe. Jack De Ford paced the long room below, his hands behind him, his face drawn and haggard. All night he had restlessly moved about from room to room, catching now and then a brief sweet glance from her tired eyes; meeting her mother in the hallway, and saying nothing, going out in the dull midnight hours on the high stoop and gazing at the dreary lamps down the street and across the park for comfort; hearing as he stood there the gentle soughing of the wind in the trees within the high iron fence; fancying spirits were whispering Florence's fate to him in words audible but incomprehensible. All the currents of his being seemed for the time stagnant and motionless. There had been long days of suspense, when his nature seemed to grow hard and cold. He had had his surfeit of sorrow, which is as fatal as a surfeit of joy. Long afterward he shuddered at such despairing emotion, and would have none of it. He had learned to avoid sorrow—to escape it.

It was five o'clock in the morning now, and the city's roar had not yet begun. The light came in slowly through the gilded blinds, and the heavy dark-green velvet curtains did their best to shut it out. What were night and day to him? He wandered about the great house, occasionally passing on the stair his elderly father-in-law, who was more bowed down and depressed than he, with his youth and health, could ever be. He was glad the doctors persisted in their cold professionalism; that the nurses were indifferent, but keenly alert. Science was battling against the destroyer Death, and Science must needs be well armed. The days and months of winter had been so happy in the old house in Gramercy Park! Life had moved along in the smoothest orbit. How easy it was, now, to make money in the street! Luck favored every turn he made. His keen, quick brain had detected and turned to his firm's advantage a great "deal" among the magnates in grain. Luck had been with him in everything so far. Was it to turn now, and punish him more deeply, more severely than if it had let him alone and given him no happiness whatever?

Then, along with his thoughts of self, came the crushing, despairing remorse of his own self being the cause of Florence's death. No amount of argument could turn his mind from this morbid self-accusation. "I am her murderer," he thought in agony. "Her love for me has been her death." The feeble red, wailing little mite of humanity which they had let him hold a moment on a dainty lace-trimmed pillow, and told him was his daughter, he regarded with absolute aversion; the child was he himself—a murderer. "Good God! Almighty God! do not let her die!" he cried, sobbing and throwing himself on a sofa. "She has always been so gentle, so sweet! She has been so good, O God! so tender to all who came within the radiance of her beauty. Must she die? Is she too pure, too exquisite?" Then he sat up a moment. He knew there was some extra excitement in the sick-room upstairs. A cab had rattled up. A learned physician—one of the profoundest of medical men in America—had been summoned from his bed. He saw him make his way upstairs—a strong-featured, silent man—accompanied by the two regular doctors. There was a long interval. He looked up suddenly. It was lighter, but the gas was still burning in the daylight, and his mother-in-law's face looked almost yellow as she came to the door timidly. He sat up and looked at her inquiringly. "She would say," he thought rapidly before she could say anything at all, "She is dead," or "There is no hope," or "She said 'Good-by, Jack,'" or she would merely sit down and cry. But Mrs. Heath said or did none of these things. She said, "She wishes to see you." De Ford rose quickly, and passed out, patting her shoulder, and saying nothing. He had a way of patting her, which she had grown to expect and like. It meant very much more to her just then than words.

A sense of his own unworthiness overburdened him again as he climbed the stairs heavily. He felt he had too much dross.

He was of the earth earthy. His soul said to his inner soul, "Am I worthy?" and received a distant and hesitating negative. He was entering into the presence of a pure young saint, who already had lived in the other world—who had been for days hardly confined in that white, pure, exquisitely moulded shell—her body. The doctors were talking together in the smaller ante-room, below a gas-burner turned on full as he entered. One was laughing. It jarred on his feelings and he nervously muttered an oath below his breath; then waited again a moment, turned, went into another room and knelt down alone, praying God, whatever happened—whatever happened, to change *him*. It was only about himself that he felt concern just then. His own shortcomings, not deep and desperate then, poor Jack, but felt overwhelmingly. He prayed like a little child, begging God, with streaming eyes, to change him for the better and concretely to change him so that he would never swear again. Poor Jack!

It is only human nature to cry out aloud at such times to this Higher Force, Power, God, or what you will. It is nature's cry, felt, instinctive, and based upon our everlasting need. Then he arose from his knees, calmer, but still timid and fearful. It had all taken but two or three moments, yet Florence said softly as he bent over her:

"I thought you were never coming, Jack—and, Jack, I have so much to say, dear. It worries me about those poor people of mine, Mrs. Jones and Mrs. Murphy and their children. When I go I can't bear to leave them to their fate. Dear, you won't let them suffer?"

"Not as long as I live, and if you go I want to go too, dear, very soon."

He was entirely sincere.

"Jack, the baby—she needs you. A girl needs her father. I don't want you to think of following me. It's perfectly absurd, it's ridiculous. I shall be provoked. Now, I won't have it! There!"

He felt her beauty as she lay there white on her white pillows, her dark hair caught by a diamond pin in a dainty Frenchy little cap of expensive lace. She had passed the point of regretting—not a difficult point with those many women whose lives are self-abnegating from childhood in all their daily, infinitely small details. Her own life—what was it? How cheaply she valued it! All the fuller, the entire life, the absolute certainty of a hereafter, was in her every glance, in her smile, so sweet that he too, as his hand ran lightly over her hair, and the tears, wrenched from his heart, suffused his eyes, dreamed that he heard music and felt himself raised up in a divine ecstasy. A man rarely reaches these divine heights, my masters. He felt silenced, humbled, quiet before this pure spirit, which he saw radiant with holy light, yet which he heard talking impulsively, lightly, as she always talked. It was not incongruous to him. He felt the spirit beneath her words. He listened and nodded, holding her hand as she spoke pressed against her breast beneath the cool linen and light eider-down bedclothes. He could not control his mind's wandering into the past and future. He did not sob now; the days of wild regret and tears were over. He sat and listened at her bedside, nodding and saying, " Yes, yes, "while she quickly ran on, " as though she were really alive," he kept saying to himself, " as though she were really alive!"

"And, Jack, about the funeral. I wish you would not let papa put in the notice, 'No flowers.' I think it's horrid. I want every one to send a flower—every one I care for, and I care for so many, Jack! As I lie here I keep counting them up, faces—so many faces—I am perfectly astonished to see how many people I like—I love. They come to me of their own accord, Jack, dear, and they say 'Good-by.' Well, I want every one to send a few flowers. Just a few. I don't want any 'floral tributes.'" She smiled. "But you know, Jack, it's April now and violets are plenty. Last fall mamma and I went to such a sweet, dear funeral of a little girl on Fifty-eighth Street—Mrs. Ridding's, you know. It was very simple, but so tender. And do—do not look too sad, too solemn —Jack, it's nothing—Jack—I—I—feel so —faint——"

"She's going!" he cried aghast, and the nurses called in the doctors hurriedly.

With blanched faces papa and mamma entered together. Poor mamma, hysterical now and sobbing out, "Florry, my baby, my little Florry!" and kneeling at her bedside. It was the baby Florence of whom she was thinking—the Florence of long ago.

His wife lay there dead-white, her eyes closed, motionless, a smile on her lips, her curly dark hair escaping from the dainty little French cap and flowing out on the pillow. The doctors pressed to her bedside, the consulting physician, a rather stern, tall, older man, standing a little back. There was a flash of an hypodermic syringe. A moment and she opened her eyes slowly. "Ah—let me go——" She sighed so wearily.

The scientist—a man profounder than he *looked* was never made—turned to the poor broken old couple. "Two years ago," he said in a whisper, "I lost my daughter by not remaining in the room at a crisis like this. I learned a lesson. Calm yourselves. I shall not leave the room to-day until I am able to assure you that she will live. I am satisfied what I say is true." The great man then coolly took off his coat as if to wrestle with death more easily. Somehow this act of his sent Jack out of the room and downstairs with a revulsion of exuberant joy. The morning was sunny, and the tulips and crocuses were nodding and calling to him from the little park. He ordered let out the two brown-haired setters in the basement, and went out for a romp in the delicious freshness of the morning. Ah, the pretty park never looked so beautiful as then! She would live! She would live!

IX.

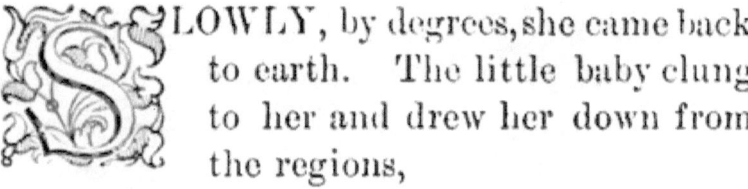LOWLY, by degrees, she came back to earth. The little baby clung to her and drew her down from the regions,

"Where the human spirit seeks for Peace."

Death hid away, then slunk away wholly overcome. Life had come—baby-life, jolly and smiling. Now with the spring came soft, balmy little airs from the tree-tops of the park, and every twittering, noisy English sparrow seemed to have a word for the sweet girl-wife of love and good cheer and good hope.

The warm, sunny day came when Florence could sit up and look out upon the world. I don't suppose her father or her mother thought at all about her beauty. If she had been a plain, homely-faced daughter (but with such a tender soul how could she have been anything but beautiful?), the two jealous, doting old people would have acted just the same. Papa said very little, but he did the queerest things during her illness. He slipped out one day and went himself to see about Mrs. Murphy and her children, of whom "Florry" was always speaking. The old gentleman did not leave them till he had spoiled the children with candy and left a twenty-dollar bill in Mrs. Murphy's hands.

We all go down once or twice in our lives into the Valley of the Shadow, stay there for a period, then come out again smiling, with somehow a new callousness born of a period of too great mental suffering. All three had a reaction now into a liking for pure rough nonsense and amusement. Night after night papa, mamma, and Jack sought out comic minstrel-shows, coarse, farce-like plays; the theatres did not furnish much else—anything *pour amuser*. The circus came in the middle of May, and no children enjoyed it more than these three. Night after night, after kissing Florence good-by and seeing her safe in bed with the baby within arm's reach, they drove to the circus and saw the frightful leaps of Monsieur Frascati and the brilliant bareback riding of Mlle. Trois-Étoiles, with an amused complacency.

It came to be the middle of June. Florence rode out now, but riding on the rough pavements tired her. She came to prefer rolling out in her wheel-chair beneath the trees in the little park; so every morning now, before the sun got very hot, a little procession started from the old house. First came the little princess in her carriage with attendant waiting-women; then the queen, her mamma, in her throne-chair and footmen; then Jack, the king, who seemed to take a trifle more notice now of the little red princess with dark eyes, who said nothing, but whose smiles were worth untold efforts in the way of baby-talk and shaking rattles. Later grandpa, the dethroned monarch, would come out into the park with his cigar and morning paper. It was curious how everything these people did was tinged with a hidden, ill-concealed hilarity. With the heart merry, what trifles please! Little sweet glances of the eye from Florence to Jack. Little laughing jokes on his enormous parental gravity! Grandpapa's heavy solemn jests, too, went very well now. He liked to appear over-brusque, over-rude, to say the roughest and toughest things of the Democratic party—to say them brutally, out of his very jollity and content. As for the city—he was going to buy a house in Dublin—there were *some* English there! He prophesied catastrophe to the country with a smiling of the lip; ruin to everybody high and low, big and little—they then realized how happy he was! He was not sure but that the prophet Jeremiah or Isaiah, Mother Shipton, or somebody was right, and the end of the world was at hand. "I have never known your father in such high spirits," said his good wife at each appalling announcement.

And it was papa, with Jack's aid, who played the remarkable practical joke on both the good mother and daughter and the little grand-daughter too, though she was so quick and smart that she caught on to it at the outset, but promised not to tell, at least until she could talk. They hired Sundown, the artist, to surreptitiously "do" the mother and child in a madonna-like portrait without their knowing it. Sundown entered into the spirit of the thing. He pretended to be making a "study" of the park for a large painting, and so Florence unconsciously posed every morning for him there. One morning he had two very successful hours of Florence innocently holding little Dorothy nestled in her arms right before him. He caught a perfect likeness of the madonna and child, for his soul responded to hers, and the rare beauty of her eyes he felt and painted as only a true artist can. "Why, pray, Mr. Sundown, do you keep looking at us so?" With Florence it was always "we" and "us" now.

"Er—you happen to be sitting just before a tree I am sketching." And Sundown, nothing abashed, brought forward the landscape and pointed out the identical tree. Florence was quite satisfied. She liked Sundown; he had frank, fine eyes; she enjoyed his conversation about Italy. He was a little bit "free" about Paris, where he had studied two years under the great Gerome. He told many stories of Meissonier, Bouguereau, of Dupré, Millet, and others.

"Such lives those wretched French artists live!" she sighed. "But about Italy—what he said was so reverent, so full of feeling!"

"I feel that we must buy Mr. Sundown's pretty picture of the park," said Florence one day. "He has entertained us delightfully. I usually have my chair wheeled near where he is painting. The only thing—I don't believe he means to be rude—but he keeps staring so——"

"Let him stare," said Jack laughing, in which odd sentiment grandpapa precipitately concurred. "He's a gentleman, and one of the best of the younger artists of the day. He likes to look at beautiful things, doesn't he?"

"He is very fond of babies; I suppose it's Dorothy he looks at," said grandpapa, with a guilty conscience.

"Let him stare," added Jack; "I shall invite him to the house. I like him. I'm going to buy some of his pictures, two Venetian studies—good work, they say. Oh, let him stare!"

So Sundown stared on and Florence gently forgave him, and believed it was the way with all artists to use their eyes. Sundown used his to a good purpose. Florence walked on her husband's arm into the drawing-room one evening; and there, lit up by a dozen candles, in a gorgeous Florentine frame—as if above an altar and making an altar-piece—she first saw the result of Sundown's work. Curious—odd folk these wives of ours! Florence stamped her little foot; she was quite provoked.

"If I had died," she said, much agitated, "such a thing might have done. It is too high—too divine. I—I am only your little Florry, Jack."

Jack said nothing, but put his arm around the sweet girl at his side. His thoughts flew back to that dreadful morning when all that was dear in life seemed slipping from his grasp. The artist had caught the divine, unselfish, unworldly "motherhood" in Florence's lovely eyes. The portrait meant a great deal to him. It was Florence's higher self—the self she kept back out of the way, afraid to expose—not the self she felt she could always day by day live up to.

"It is to me—everything," he muttered. "It helps me so," and he was silent.

"Shall I ever dare to frivol with that thing in the house?" she whispered. "Shall I ever dare to laugh, to romp about? Jack, I don't want to be *very* good; I don't want to be better than you!"

He laughed and kissed her.

"I mean I—you are—you don't want me to be like that?"

He blew out the candles one by one. When they were all out and they stood in the semi-darkness holding each other's hands, he whispered: "I want always to remember that you are my good angel; lots of times I forget. I am cross. I am tired. I am worried with business. I am forgetful of you. Long before those dreadful days when Dorothy came, and after, I had not thought of you to love you as I did suddenly that morning we thought you were gone. Then—then it was different. A man's wife should sink into him for all time and simply be him—his higher soul. High, high up, I enshrine you, dear."

"Jack—I—I just won't!"

She threw herself, happy, into his arms. It was a moment of sublime unselfish love on both sides—a moment of supreme exaltation of spirit, when the earthly dross has, as it seemed, wholly fallen away. She kissed her husband, and said that the portrait should after all be a pattern for her to live up to. "For us both and Dorothy," she said.

Ah, the world—the world! Would that these two could have gone together into Elysium then! The world became cruel to them later on, and the portrait was destined to look down on much sorrow and many tears.

X.

"AH, Jack, I can't go away and leave you alone all summer."

"It is best."

"But it has never happened before."

"No—you have Dorothy now to love."

She gazed at him reproachfully.

"And I have the portrait," he laughed.

Suddenly she sprang upon him, seizing him almost fiercely by the arm. Loving women occasionally do these things.

"Do you love me now, Jack?" she panted.

He burst out laughing. "Seriously," he added soothingly, "Dorothy must get up into the mountains at once. Here it is almost July. What are we thinking of. Ourselves—our love? We must think of Dorothy."

"Well, then, I shall go to Lawrence or Seabright—or where it will be near you——"

"No, the doctors say the mountains. They are right, dear. We must be content to be separated for the child's sake. I have taken a cottage in Franconia. Everything is arranged. I can come up Sundays——"

"Tell me, Jack, is this the way all married people in New York who have children have to do? Oh, I hate our horrid climate, which compels us to do this!"

"They call it the 'Annual Divorce' at the club," he laughed.

"It's wrong, it's wicked!" she kept saying, feeling instinctively that she could not bear to allow anything to come in and prevent her sharing her husband's daily life.

But after a day or so of unusual heat, Florence yielded to persuasion, and July was spent in the mountains in keenest fresh air, the best of food, the best of Alderney milk, the best of care for mother and child. Florence, during the long summer days while Jack was in the city, to amuse herself, took up French again. She read Gasparin, Pascal, Du Guérin. She spent days lying on the grass under the trees with Dorothy near by. The blue skies and white dreamy clouds floated above her. She had little social gayety. She was at peace.

Their cottage, not far from the hotel, surmounted a knoll from which was a distant view of Bethlehem and the Franconia Mountains. The summer wind came to them from across a wide stretch of valley, laden with the sweet clover perfumes and the musky smell of hay. The world—the whole earth—seemed far distant, far below. Unconsciously Florence grew in appearance in certain ways more and more like her portrait. Her mother remarked it.

"When Jack comes up next Sunday——"

"Three whole days off, mamma——"

"He will say that Mr. Sundown has not overdone the "dreamy" look, Florry. You are too lonely here. You are very pensive." She meant, poor soul, it was becoming stupid for *her* there with so little social life. "You are so content; but remember, Florry, you are still in the world, my child. There were Mr. and Mrs. Chutney at the hotel last week. We should have called."

"I have been selfish. We will have a tea-party."

Mrs. Heath could not conceal her pleasure. She took the baby up and "clucked" and "guggled" to it.

"I did not want to be the one to suggest it," she said, "but I think it would be a good idea—an excellent idea. There are the Richmonds, the Lockerts, the Bradleys, at the hotel; and I'm very fond of Mrs. Bradley, who has a new crochet-stitch."

Florence gave a little sigh. "Dorothy is so all in all to me, that I am forgetful," she said; "I live in the new world of babyland. Of course we must invite them; as for men, Mrs. Chutney said that Mr. Sundown was expected."

"No one expects men to be away from business, but Mr. Sundown shall be made to do double duty. Is he really coming up to the mountains? That will be so nice! I am fond of Mr. Sundown. We must make him talk about Italy. We must shut him off about Paris. But there must be some more men? Mamma, pray go and run your eye over the hotel register to-day. Certainly we must have a tea, and we can have it Saturday night, when Jack and papa are here."

"Friday would be better. Your father does not enjoy teas. Friday it must be, Florence. Do you think after riding in the cars all day they will enjoy talking to ladies?"

Florence pondered a moment. "Mr. Sundown will be our only man, then?" she said.

"He is enough. He is very talkative. He will be a belle. But Mrs. Locker is quite manlike too. She has such a deep voice! Besides, there is old Colonel Bradley."

"We could telegraph that we intended to have the tea, and if they could tear themselves away from business they could come up."

"Oh, yes, we can do that; but they won't come. Your father never likes to leave before Saturday, and Jack is very much like your father."

Mrs. Heath fanned herself gently. She had paid Jack the highest compliment she was capable of. Florence had not noticed it. Suddenly the elder sprang up. "I forgot that we fare at the mercy of our servants up here," she said; "I must go and ask them."

Florence gazed after her mother as she busily trotted off into the house. Some one entered the gate. It was Sundown, looking bronzed and very handsome in his artistic velveteens and knickerbockers. He bowed, praised the baby in a few commonplaces, and at once entered into conversation about Italy. It was an Italian sky, an Italian haze, an Italian sunset last night. He had observed, too, a number of Italian gentlemen at work upon the railroad that morning.

"Ah, and how is *bambina?*" he asked, leaning over Dorothy's basket-carriage, while Florence laughed. "And how is Madonna?" he added.

"That is the bone I have to pick with you, Mr. Sundown; you have actually canonized me."

"I—I am no ecumenical council rolled into one," he laughed.

"But the portrait—how can I ever live up to it?" She made an expressive grimace.

He looked down on her upturned face a moment and said nothing. "Is it too good?" he asked at length. "Can it be? Ah, well, it is *you*, Mrs. De Ford, as you seem to me." Then he added to himself: "If you were not so pure and high I should dare love you. I should taint you by daring to love you; as it is, I may only worship with the throng!"

"You must come to our tea Friday, Mr. Sundown," said she. "It is a very formal affair, you must understand, and you must expect to make yourself very entertaining. You and Colonel Bradley will be the only men."

"Colonel Bradley!"

"He is available, and I admire his white

hair and white mustachios; therefore, he shall come to our tea."

"Ah, yes, certainly. But I am rather timid. You will let me devote myself to you and Dorothy?"

"We will not do anything of the sort. We shall expect him to make himself especially agreeable to our guests—shan't we, Dorothy, dear?"

Dorothy gave an amiable little coo as her mother kissed her fat cheeks.

"And he mustn't say that teas disagree with him, as papa does."

"Oh, I am perfectly willing to be teased by teas," laughed Sundown, lazily throwing himself on the close-cut grass. "Now isn't that a perfect Venetian blue sky across the valley beyond the mountains? I remember once in a gondola—Miss Franscioli was very handsome, but I despise a woman who flirts —don't you, Mrs. De Ford? I mean who openly, unguardedly flirts; uses her eyes, smiles—don't you, Mrs. De Ford?"

"How unkind of you to ask; let my portrait speak," she replied sedately.

"Miss Franscioli had been a Mrs. Franscioli, of New Orleans (a rich banker); then a Mrs. Miles, of Chicago."

"How odd! I don't understand."

"The divorce courts had turned her back into a Miss—a Miss is as good as a mile, you know. She is as young and as handsome, and flirtations as ever; and in Venice, two years ago—her party was at my hotel on the Grand Canal—she and I struck up, or rather, renewed our acquaintance made in Washington a few years ago. She was not then the facinating *divorcée* she is now. She was rather quiet and fond of her child, who since died suddenly in Paris."

"Oh, she had a child, and she——"

"Oh, well, she was too handsome and too fond of the world, don't you know, to leave it permanently. She has mourned a year after the little girl's death; but a friend told me she was gayer than ever in Washington last season, and that illustrates my idea."

"What dreadful idea is that, Mr. Sundown?"

Florence was always interested in what the young artist had to say. She leaned forward now, and glanced at him with an amused smile. He stared at her as frankly as ever he had done in Gramercy Park. It was a sudden influx of the world Mr. Sundown had brought with him—the great world she had so lost sight of amid the hills and clover-fields of the high Hampshire uplands with her little Dorothy.

"My idea is," he said, "that people are sometimes made harder by sorrows—are more stolid by going through severe crises. One is always reading the opposite of this in the novels. But trials are not good for some men. They do not come out from them stronger, but harder."

"Well, about this Miss or Mrs. Franscioli?"

"Her child's death—I think it has not done her any good."

"She must be a wretch."

"On the contrary, I wish she could meet you, you would say she was very charming. She is, in fact, a gorgeous woman. She has dark reddish hair, such as Rubens loved to paint; eyes literally flashing. Indeed, Mrs. De Ford, they seemed, as I remember, to throw out a certain light."

Mrs. Heath came out on the lawn under the apple trees just then, and Sundown arose and saluted her politely.

"You are coming, of course, Friday?" she asked, as she smiled upon him with her calm, patient eyes. He murmured an assent, and a half-hour later sauntered leisurely away down the hill, thinking how lovely the young mother looked in her pretty white morning robe against the clover green. His artist eye did not altogether relish the Queen Anne cottage with the washing hanging out, indicative of Mary Ann in the rear; but he forgave much in the presence of the woman he had begun to worship as from afar.

XI.

SUNDOWN carried the picture of the thick-leaved, shady apple tree in the grassy meadow, the sweet young wife propped up on pillows beneath it, the baby lying in her lap, the amiable kindly grandmother standing behind her—for many a day. It remained after many other pictures had come to his mental vision in after days. There was a "roundness" in all of Florence's attitudes which caught his artist eye. Her dark hair filled in the delicious little hollow of her neck in a most charming way. The white dress became her; the pillows of damask silk, the high-colored rugs on the grass, the tree above, "thick-leaved, ambrosial," her little feet showing their dainty-slippered tips. She would have sat to a better portrait in the mountains, he thought, than the one which hung in the old house in Gramercy Park. She was still ill, then; she was paler; she looked more like some happy saint. It was a good piece of work, the portrait, however.

His artist friends spoke in highest praise of it. Ah, how he would have loved to paint her now—a woman, not a saint, with heart and feeling and human life speaking in her face!

Pretending he wished to sketch a bit of mountain from just exactly that spot, he came to spend his days there, talking and chatting to the mother and daughter, four days until Friday night came, and with it their eventful tea.

Only very foolish people may connect Friday, hangman's day, the 13th of the month, the night of their tea, with any superstitious feeling. The night of the day before papa had received a telegram at the house in Gramercy Park, announcing their little function, and begging him to come up a day ahead. He had hastily answered it: "Cannot leave biz. Very sorry."

When Jack came home later from business he read their telegram and said, "I believe I'll go up and surprise them."

"Go, by all means," said his father-in-law; "I can't get away. It's my busy time, you know, in leather. Buy a lot of knick-knacks at Dourbley's and take up; they'll like them for their tea."

"I can go just as well as not. The market is very dull," yawned De Ford. "But I know this; if I do go something is sure to happen in the street, and I shall be needed, as Mr. Beach and Mr. Catherly are away now. However," and he thought of his wife and of Dorothy under the shady apple trees on the sloping lawn, "I guess I'll chance it."

The day was hot when he started. There was a great deal of unnecessary delay over a freight train which had been thrown off the track at Springfield. His train was an hour and a half late. The dinner he got at a railway station was anything but satisfactory. When he arrived at last at Franconia, he jumped into a hack and drove home rapidly in the sweet early evening, regretting now the fact of the tea and strangers and the need of being polite, when he hungered and thirsted only to see his wife and his child. There was a moon above the horizon, and near it a star, Venus. The moon hung like a lamp above the mountains in the pinkish light left from the sunset. The mountains were a deep rich violet. High up above him, across an upland field, he saw his cottage lights twinkling, and thought he heard music. He only heard the krick-krick of the locusts, the chirp of the crickets, the whistle of the locomotive of his fast receding train; but the whole scene filled him with unutterable longing to clasp his wife in his arms—gave him a lover's fear that she might be ill—

"A sense of dread, lest she be dead."

He hastily paid the driver his fare, jumped out, and struck out on a run cross-lots to his house.

"That 'ere man's in a hurry, I guess," said Mr. Higgins, the driver, looking vaguely after him; "most o' them husbands like to hang around the tavern a leetle while afore goin' home, but he don't. Wal, Mr. De Ford, he's jest married, an' he ain't ben up fer two weeks. Wal, that 'caounts fer it," and he slowly turned his old horse around.

At the side of the cottage was a garden and small summer-house, covered with vines and clematis and honeysuckle; leading out to it was a path through the garden, lined with currant-bushes.

De Ford was obliged to clamber up a sharp ascent over rocks and to dodge around boulders, but he knew the path and he had no serious difficulty in picking it out. He cared not, then, for bruised shins! He neared the house, saw people on the wide veranda, heard the jingly piano played while a lady sang. There were two people standing in the summer-house, a woman and a tall man. He crept close enough to see it was his wife. She was standing near the man in the pale moonlight, and they were laughing together and looking at the beautiful moon and the star.

De Ford felt a sudden strange revulsion of feeling. He paused and stood still, where just before he felt like shouting a joyous view-hallo; he hid behind some bushes, then made a circuit and came up in front of the cottage on the gravel path. The first one he saw was his mother-in-law, but for some reason he would not kiss her. Inside the drawing-room came out to him the "infernal buzz" of conversation; he refused to enter. When Florence, radiant with love and happy laughter, came hurrying in, he just barely touched her forehead with his lips.

"Mr. Sundown is here, Jack," she said; "isn't it nice?"

He turned away and frowned. He felt that he was angry because she was not watching and waiting for *him*, and thinking of him alone, just as he felt her portrait in the old city house kept its eyes always for him alone whenever he came home. "Some day," he said, "I'll punish her for this! Ah, how tanned she is; she is not quite the same—she is changed!"

Florence stood looking at him in surprise. Absence had but made *her* heart grow fonder.

XII.

BY the time that every one was gone Jack recovered himself. It seemed to the girl's discerning instinct that he was fiercer, wilder in his demonstrativeness than ever before. She felt that something had happened. His kisses burned like fire. He frightened her.

"I know, I know," she kept saying. "I hate surprises, and they always end badly. I was not here when you came in. I was not the first one you saw. It was too bad, Jack; but really, under the circumstances——"

"Oh, don't apologize," he laughed. "Does Mr. Sundown 'stare' as much as ever? If he does, I shall tell him to his face that now the portrait is done it is a decided impertinence. Pray, how long has he been here? These artists, they can tolly-diddle all summer over the rocks and the hills and never a question asked!"

Then he saw his wife looked pained, and he stopped abruptly.

"I hope Mr. Heath is well, and will be up to-morrow," ventured his mother-in-law, placidly.

"Yes, he will be——"

Jack seemed to be thinking of something. He was absent-minded, *distrait*. But Florence was too happy now to notice it. She went at him now after the manner of wives whom fate compels to be absent from husband and city shops through the long vacation of summer. "Did you bring up the lilac silk I ordered?"

"Yes."

"Did you see about the brown holland covers for the furniture?"

"Yes."

"Did you get baby's little silk shirts?"

"Yes."

"Did you remember to bring the medicine from Dr. Chesney?"

"Yes."

"Did you see to the moths in the top bureau drawers in the rear chamber? Oh, Jack!"

"No—I—I—I forgot that."

Florence got up and walked out of the room, saying: "Jack, dear, how could you be so forgetful? All baby's winter underclothing will be eaten up."

He heard his wife go into the little parlor and run over a few provoked little bars on the piano. He took out a cigar, lit it, and went out into the calm moonlit night. For the first time in many days he said below his breath, "*Damn!*" and then he burst out laughing.

XIII.

BUT the next day brought the rich peace and calm of the mountains into his heart. He lay, his head in Florence's lap, his hair fondly patted by her white hand, while she read him a charming story, just then out, of Howells. The child, Dorothy, doubled her little fists into her puckery little mouth near at hand, while her French *nou-nou* in all the glorious nurse habiliments of Paris—the long cap-ribbons and the long purple cloak—sat near by on the grass with a cow-like placidity, gazing at the distant hills. Florence was fortunate in being able to nurse the child herself. The French girl, a huge creature with the jolliest laugh in the world, had now very little to do; but her smile, for provoking contentment, was worth her wage.

Presently Florence put down her book and gazed calmly off at the mountains.

"Mrs. Locker was saying last night," she said, "that this annual separation for the summer, of husbands and wives, was such a blessing."

"Humph, I don't know," said Jack drowsily.

"I think it makes us appreciate each other all the more, Jack—don't you think?"

Jack sat up. The subject interested him.

He scratched his head. Then he laid down, vehemently, this formula:

"*A man and wife ought never to be separated a day.*"

Florence looked at him wonderingly. "Necessity," she murmured, "Dorothy."

"Every day, every hour, we grow, change, we look at things differently. We have fads and fancies. Temporary separation is called a short death; so it is apt to be—of constancy."

He was thinking of the picture Sundown and she made together in the vine-clad arbor. The picture was framed in his mind to stay, as it seemed. Poor Jack!

"Constancy!" she cried half-surprised, and applying his words personally. "Must I be always in New York, Jack, to keep your love for me up to the scratch? Oh, Jack!"

"Men are apt to be even less tempted than

their wives, I think, because they are busy." He said this nonchalantly, in an easy tone.

"As if I were not busy!" laughed Florence, showing all her white, pretty teeth. "From morning to night I am just as busy with baby as I can be, and I sing lullabies about 'Father will come to thee soon,' don't I, baby? And I—I—Jack, I think you are just as cruel as you can be!"

There was a suspicion of tears in her pretty eyes.

He could not bring himself then to mention Sundown's name. It is needless to say it did not enter the mind of the beautiful girl-wife at his side. He got up, yawned, and stretched himself, as a man will do when he comes out from the city and breathes anew the sweet perfume of the fields, ripening now for the harvest. He caught up the baby and tossed it, and said a great quantity of nonsense to it. He told it a great deal about the loneliness of New York, the dulness of life in the "metropolis," and the nobility of man toiling to bedizen his wife and child with precious stones through the torrid, infernal heats of a cloudless August.

Florence caught the little belaced and beflounced bit of humanity from him, and kissing it again and again, and told it of the delights of club-life, the theatres, the sea-bathing for a city man, and solemoly called its attention to the "poky" stupidity of life on a hill, where one was only to be stared at by an occasional cow.

The use of the words "stared at" was unfortunate. It brought an unpleasant train of thought to De Ford's quick, supersensitive mind. He turned away, and without a word strolled down and out the road toward the hotel.

"Jack, where are you going?" called out Florence after him.

"I'm going in search of that cow," he called back without smiling.

She turned slowly and went back into the house. Our Othello walked with his hands thrust into his pockets, his brows knit, saying and muttering to himself: "What a stupid fool I am to question the sincerity and love of that dearest girl on earth! Can't I see her talking with another man without being an ass?"

His anti-conscience—for men have two voices—spoke up and said: "Ah, but you would have liked it better if there had not been that other man. Of course you don't doubt her heart. It is yours; but she has listened to the ideas of another than you."

Himself: "So she may—in books."

His Anti-conscience: "No, but it is the man that she first feels behind his ideas. Such is woman's nature. *She* is especially susceptible."

His Conscience: "She is noble and good. She loves me wholly, utterly. I may not question her. Go back now to her, *thou!* Take her in *my* arms and love her."

He went to the side of the road and took out his knife to cut an alder stick. While he was hidden in the bushes an open carriage passed. There were some ladies: Mrs. Locker, Mrs. Colonel Bradley, and another. As they went by, he heard one of them say in a loud, masculine voice:

"Why, he is there every day, all day long."

"I didn't think Mr. Sundown was that sort of a man," replied another, and the carriage passed on.

Jack did not cut the alder. He sat drearily on the fence a few moments, while his conscience said:

"You are doing wrong to distrust her slightest thought."

He returned home, inwardly in a state of keenest sadness, outwardly a little pale and looking rather old. Florence had gone upstairs with Dorothy. Presently he heard her singing softly:

> "Sweet and low,
> Sweet and low.
> Father will come to thee soon."

"Idiot that I am to torment myself for nothing," he said so savagely that Mrs. Heath looked up from her paper surprised.

"What is the matter, Jack?" she asked.

"People are not stationary," he insisted vaguely.

"I have heard your father say that there were a great many paper men in the world." She looked up and caught his amused smile. It was an innocent little trick of hers to speak to him of her husband as "your father."

"People fluctuate — change," he said. "Nothing remains long the same We Americans crave new pleasures, new excitements, and with women—of course it must be so. I'm an idiot, that's all, mother."

She looked at him with an expression of utter lack of comprehension.

He ran his eye over the shelf of books

above the wide brick mantel, and took down one, "Taylor's Holy Living and Dying." She looked up very much reassured, as he added inconsequently, "Sundown is very much of a gentleman: let's have him dine with us to-morrow, by all means."

XIV.

IN September De Ford gave himself a vacation of a few weeks, and he persuaded Florence to take the baby and its paraphernalia down to the seaside. He proposed going to Rye Beach, which was not so many miles away, and going by carriage in easy stages. As he would be with her now it mattered not where they went seaward, and so they had determined upon the wide level shore of Rye. Florence put against the plan all her mother's, all her woman's fears. The dangers to baby were recounted again and again. The dangers of storms, of crossing railway tracks, the dangers of bridges, of swollen streams, and oh—if Dorothy were to be kidnapped!

"Who would want such a little red Indian?" he laughed.

"Who would want her?" cried Florence, flying at her child and snatching it to her bosom. "The whole world wants her! The naughty, horrid everybody!" And she fell to kissing the little mite with great unction.

Dorothy set up a wail of protest. No young and jealous parent is ever so pleased as when the infant cries proceed from some indiscretion on the part of the other parent.

"Let *me* take her," laughed Jack, reaching out his hands. "You don't know how to treat her with the dignity she deserves."

Florence bridled a little. It was quite true that the fickle Dorothy was always willing to leave her mamma for her papa's strong arms. She stretched out her arms now, and ceased her wails at once.

"Yes, she doesn't see you every day and night; she doesn't get tired of you as she does of me."

"As if any one could ever get tired of you, my sweetheart," he said impulsively, with a sudden accession of kindness.

Florence smiled very sweetly. She was a woman who seemed to grow and shine like a rare flower in happiness. Gentle thoughts always pervaded her; but they rose to the surface oftener when she felt her husband's love and bathed in its glory, as it were.

"It is these long absences from you and Dorothy that I dislike so much," he said.

"Ah, Florry, we ought never to be away from each other an instant, not an instant."

"When do we start for the seashore?" she asked, for her opposition had now melted away.

"Day after to-morrow."

"So soon?"

Her nervous, restless husband gave her the baby to hold and lit a cigarette. "Why not?" he said. "I want to get on the move. I mean to take three days in going a hundred miles. It will be a grand cavalcade, a sort of royal progress, a caravan. There will be our carriage, the baggage-wagon, and the old folks' carriage. I've arranged it all—where we stop each night, and where we picnic along the road, for lunch, under the trees. It will be great fun."

She saw that he was delighted with his plans, and she entered into them with a fictitious glee. Inwardly she feared all manner of things, animate and inanimate, from runaway horses down to mad dogs.

Yet when the "day after to-morrow" came and the cavalcade started (the older couple were great enthusiasts for this carriage journey), Florence put on a brave countenance. In the first place she held Dorothy close in her arms, and a woman with her child is afraid of nothing concrete that actually confronts her. In the second place she looked at the slow old horses, at faithful old Mr. Higgins, their driver, and was reassured when he said solemnly:

"Them brutes'd rayther lay daown an' roll 'n draw five folks the hull way ter Rye."

"Five folks—four folks," said Florence quickly.

"Me an' you, the nuss, Mr. De Ford, an' the babby is jest five," he maintained stoutly.

"Oh, the baby!" she laughed, very much pleased. Little things made her happy in these days.

"Why them harses is mos' old 's I be," he added. "Don't hev no fears, mum; I'm a-drivin' this 'ere barooch. I'm a-drivin' it slow a puppus. We ain't goin' fer to race daown. We're goin' ter take it easy—so g'long!"

Papa and mamma drove their own team, a comfortable wide buggy with a pair of young and lively horses. It was not considered by Mr. Higgins as stylish a turn-out as their own, for "barooches" were a rarity in the mountains. The lively young horses carried the old people along at a rapid gait, and Mr.

Heath, who was always a stickler for promptness, was always "ready and waitin'" for them at the end of the day's trip.

Days of great happiness they were, "a royal progress," Jack called it—a progress diversified by many halts, by lunches under the sheltering forest trees, by little baths *au pieds* in the cool mountain-brooks. They slowly drew by the many clean little farms, the full barns, the wide pastures containing dainty, sleek cattle. They slept in comfortable country inns on feather beds, and even ate the tough country fried steaks with relish.

Nearly every one passed them on the road and smiled, but they were a little rolling world in themselves and cared not. They were happy then.

They never felt afterward quite such happiness, such isolation. The third day they drew within sight and smell of the sea, and the cool, salty breath coming across the wide flats raised Dorothy's thin little curls and cooled their own brows.

"*Ciel!*" cried the French *nou-nou*, "*la belle mer!*" It was almost the first word she had spoken. She loved the sea, as all Normandy French peasant women do. They had not regarded her presence especially on the front seat before them. They believed their affection was untranslatable in the French. Happy days, indeed, when their stolid, smiling, staring nurse did not prevent a hasty occasional kiss.

So they accomplished their descent from the mountains, and came out upon the sandy shores of Rye.

They were not, however, to be entirely without adventure. As they approached the little village on the sea a horse carrying a lady came dashing madly down the road toward them. Jack quickly jumped out before his wife could detain him, and, seizing a rail of the fence, held it across the runaway's path. It brought the horse to a standstill in short order.

The lady merely thanked De Ford coolly and rather disdainfully, and, whipping her steed again into a furious canter, passed on as if she had not been running away at all.

Afterward they knew the young lady as a "Miss Franscioli."

"She's either a mad woman or she's utterly tired of life," was Jack's comment at the time.

7

Florence, whose heart had been in her throat, cried on his shoulder. "Jack, Jack! would you have killed yourself for *her*, dear? Did you not think of *us*?"

XV.

THE hotel where they had taken a suite of rooms was a large one recently built, and there was a ball every night. It was now well filled with guests returning from the mountain resorts, and from the numerous watering-places along the northern Maine coast. The warm weather continued late, and detained many a family from returning to their city home.

One morning Jack did not go down on the sands with them, as usual. Florence looked back inquiringly and observed him sitting in a group of fashionably-dressed ladies and gentlemen on the piazza. Presently a tall lady arose and came down the steps, and he followed her. They caught up with Florence as she and the nurse, carrying Dorothy, were slowly meandering to the shore. The tall young lady was very handsome, and had the patrician air of a *grand dame*. She was dressed elegantly in a morning gown of white crêpe; she wore a large hat, covered with flowers.

"Miss Franscioli, I want you to know my wife," said Jack.

"I'm delighted to meet you," said Miss Franscioli, grasping Florence's hand with the high elbow shake. "After what Mr. Sundown has said of you, I feel I have already half-made your acquaintance. He came down here, as you have done, from the mountains, and he could talk of no one but his 'Madonna.'"

As she spoke Miss Franscioli turned and smiled at De Ford, who flushed a little and twirled his mustachios. She had a sinuous, wasp waist, and she held herself very erect, inclining her head to one side, which oddly gave her a slightly deprecatory air. She smiled and let her white sun-umbrella fall on her shoulder tentatively.

"I have heard Mr. Sundown speak of you, Mrs. Franscioli."

"It is *Miss* Franscieli," muttered De Ford correctingly, and coughing a little.

"Oh," she laughed, "it is a matter of complete indifference to me what I am called. Every one knows my history. It has been in the newspapers. It is public property both in Chicago and elsewhere. I am a *divorcée*, Mrs. De Ford, and I am yet but twenty-two." The frankness of the young woman had its vast embarrassment for Florence.

"I am very—sorry," she murmured.

"Oh, you need not be sorry," she laughed gayly, making sport of it. "My divorce was a happier event than my marriage. But I did not come out in the sun here to talk about myself. I came out to see that beautiful baby. Do let us walk on and catch up with it!"

No one spoke then of the incident of the runaway horse the morning of their arrival. De Ford had spoken of it, but found he was considered a fool for his pains, as Miss Franscioli had a way of racing her thoroughbred along the level sandy roads at top speed.

"Dorothy is hardly six months," said Florence apologetically, "it's but a wee little thing." But she was pleased to have Dorothy made much of.

"Oh, it's such a little pretty sing!" cooed Miss Franscioli, as the smiling *nou-nou* stopped and held Dorothy out at arm's-length, for the lady to admire.

If there was anything artificial in Miss

Franscioli's raptures they did not perceive it. Florence said afterward that she did not offer to take it in her arms.

"But what of that?" replied Jack; "it does not always bespeak insincerity in a woman not to grab and tumble up a baby?" He was jealous for Dorothy, too; but did half the women at the hotel who raved over her offer to take her? Nonsense!

Florence was not strong enough to walk very far on the sands that morning, but Jack wanted some exercise, and he looked around to Miss Franscioli, asking her if she cared to walk.

"Yes," she said decidedly, "and I bathe at twelve o'clock. I don't care how cold the water is. I plunge in and plunge out again. It gives me a splendid glow from my neck to my heels. I could run you a race then, though you do look like an athlete, Mr. De Ford." She scanned him critically.

"He *was* at college," said Florence proudly. "What was your record, Jack? A hundred feet in eleven seconds?"

"Just about," said De Ford sarcastically, making a grimace.

Miss Franscioli laughed. "Oh, you fine athletic young Americans and Englishmen!

I wish I were a man! I'd like to beat you all in a foot-race."

Florence looked somewhat startled, while Jack laughed. She amused him very much. She seemed such a good fellow! She seemed so healthy also. It was a relief to be with a woman who required no assistance every step or two. How she swung off with him on the smooth shore, leaving her sun-umbrella sticking in the sands! What a glow in her passionate, handsome face! What an intoxication in her voice! Her eyes had a flash in them. He made her walk very fast, too—out of a spirit of mischief. When they were at the farthest point from the hotel and quite out of sight from Florence, she flung herself on the white, dry sands in the sun.

"Sit here a moment," she begged him laughingly, "you have winded me." . . . After a little quick breathing-pause: "Tell me, that is a beautiful wife of yours. She has distinction. But I see she does not like me."

"I think you wrong her; every one must like you."

"She doesn't like the 'Miss,'" and Miss Franscioli made a pretty pout, as if it were but a small matter.

"That is where I beg leave to differ with her, then. I think the 'Miss' is very piquant; it is very brave."

She looked at him carefully. Yes, he deliberately meant it. He intended to make her a compliment.

"Oh, if you knew what I have suffered— what my life has been! It is a fancy of mine to keep my former husband's name, yet just 'Miss' it."

"You will not keep it long," he laughed.

Another compliment! "There is something to this handsome young Benedict, after all, who so bravely stopped my horse," she said to herself.

"Wild horses could not drag me into another such *mésalliance*. No! I will now live and die an old maid!"

De Ford was amused. "She is free and outspoken with me," he thought, "because I am an old married man, and because she is so Western. She can say what she likes." He enjoyed her confidences, begun so soon, although he had only met her the night before, and spoken with her a brief half-hour in company with a number of New York people he knew at the hotel, on the wide veranda. After a little she rose abruptly and sauntered back, talking all the while rapidly, and telling him so many things about herself—as if he cared. When they reached the little group (the old people had now joined them) she was talking to him about stocks, and asking his advice about investments. She had just had twenty-five thousand dollars come in from a paid-up mortgage. What should she do with it—how invest it? She had heard of his Wall Street firm—it was well known all over the country.

"If you will wait till I get back to town, I can take care of it," he said immensely flattered.

"Oh, will you?" She fairly clapped her hands until her rings jingled. She had pretty hands, very long and ladylike, and she made much use of them. Altogether she was a woman of *ton* and beauty. In fact, all the men at Rye were fascinated by Miss Franscioli. All the women viewed her with a faint suspicion.

"She is so brave and frank, she's so honest," said the men.

"It's bravado," said the women.

"She is no hypocrite," said the husbands.

"She is artfully artless," said the wives.

To begin with, Miss Franscioli played billiards, and had been seen at a late hour in a quiet corner to smoke a cigarette. The women at once pronounced her terribly *risqué*. She followed this up by being a dashing rider and a daring swimmer. She announced that she was an athlete, and that she believed in nothing *au fin du siècle*. The women at this were in consternation. But at this juncture Mrs. Berrian Deland, of New York, arrived from Mt. Desert. Mrs. Berrien Deland was a noted woman in society, and she openly patronized and applauded Miss Franscioli. So after that she was tolerated, and even admired. They began to say of her that this wild creature delighted in showing her worst side, in putting always her worst foot foremost — that she was not really so bad. Mrs. Deland had known her very well in Washington. She had much to say of her heroic conduct toward young Picton, the senator's son. The lad was wildly in love with her, but she had sent him flying.

Indeed, she had sent many men flying. It was true — she admitted it — she never intended to marry again. But she was to be a personage, fascinating, intellectual, brilliant, overpowering! Florence was instinctively afraid of her. After a week she longed to get away from Rye. She was ready to go back to New York. Jack seemed so odd, so different there. He was always laughing and joking with Miss Franscioli. Once or twice she went upstairs to bed and cried herself to sleep. She said nothing to her mother, to any one—except to Dorothy. Jack was so thoughtless! The passionate outbursts she poured into the baby's little pink ears! Poor, astonished little Dorothy, she often wailed in protesting response!

They had been so happy in the high, pure, sweet air of the mountains; and now, if Jack would only stay by her side a minute, they would be so happy here! She loved the sea; the surf in the moonlight was simply grand at Rye. What reproachful glances she looked at him!

One day he laughed: "Now be amiable, Florry; let me have a good time. It's my outing. I like to have a little freedom. Must I sit and read to you all day? Remember, I am going back to work soon. I want all the exercise and riding I can get. Remember, dear, I love you, always—always. But remember, too, my darling, that I am still half a boy. Let me play and amuse myself a little."

Miss Franscioli confided in her too, and Florence could not help pitying her. Her gayety was largely fictitious. She had had an unhappy, unsatisfied life. "Do you know what it is to have had so much despair that your whole soul is scorched into a dull, hard shell?" she asked. "That is the way with me. What do I care for anything or anybody now? 'The world's mine oyster, which I with my wit will open.' If I was a man I would have said 'sword.' I wish I were a man! I would like to fight."

To Florence it was all incomprehensible. Miss Franscioli was so outside all her reckoning! Still she found an excuse to pity her in it all. She was evidently far from being happy. She was just a little too hectic, too excitable. She was very rich, however, and made a display of her Paris toilets, which attracted immense feminine attention. Her figure was excellent. She was a graceful dancer. She was still young and at times could cleverly act the *ingènue*. She had lived in the rich, plastic society of Chicago, and had danced till morning in the gay carnival balls of St. Louis and New Orleans. At seventeen she rode on a car as "Venus" in the Mardi Gras. She was "old" then. She knew the rich, rough, passionate Western world. It is presumable that she led the staid French banker, Franscioli, a merry dance for two years. The men knew all about her at Rye. There was one thing about the Franscioli—she concealed nothing. She was altogether too frank. She was so gay, charming, full of *espièglerie*, *chic*, bravado. She loved to be advertised. She said herself that she was going back to Paris; she had already spent a season there as the beautiful bride of M. Franscioli, of New Orleans. She was going back to Paris to make one of the true *au fin du siècle* set. She was taking her farewell of America. But finally, one day, Louise Franscioli took a sudden fancy for Tuxedo—it was a letter from a dear friend of hers, who had written describing all the glories of the coming fall season. She went away impulsively with hardly any announcement, alone, with her maid. She liked to do these things.

After she was gone Florence had no further reason to shed tears alone with Dorothy as a *confidante*. Jack became very devoted, but Rye soon became an intolerable bore to him. A week later they arrived, for good and all, in Gramercy Park.

The old house never looked dearer to her. "Ah," she exclaimed, as she entered, "I wish things were different in New York! Why is the climate so wicked? Why do we ever have to go away and be homeless? The park is prettier—yes, than Franconia! The trees are quite as green, and it would not be dull here with you, Jack." She looked at her husband wistfully.

"See it in August," he laughed. "See the sun baking the brown stone into a dingy yellow; feel the heavy hot air surging out of the dense over-populated east side; note the pungent and deadly odor of the ailanthus trees. But it's a pity, though, that we can't move the house bodily away to some spot where we could live summer and winter. As I have often said, we ought never to be separated—never!" And he kissed her.

XVI.

I MEAN never to go away from him —never again, no matter how hot it may be; no matter how Dorothy may need a change. We will take a cottage near the city. If it is necessary, the house here may be sold, and we can all go where it is possible to live in one's own home the year around."

Mamma was getting used to these little confidences from Florence. She paid little attention to them generally. Now she said: "It was not the way in my time. I never left your father to melt alone through July and August—never! In September we usually went for two or three weeks on a trip out West or to Boston, where your father's family were."

"Oh, mamma, if it were only so in these days! Is New York hotter than then? Why do wives desert their husbands as they do? It is wrong! It is wrong!" she cried passionately; "Jack used to say so himself."

"It isn't the heat," said mamma. "It's cool enough—country-houses are never quite so cool in summer—but it is so debilitating. Men move about—go down to their offices; it doesn't affect them especially, but women who are forced to stay grow thin and pale indoors."

The question came up at dinner a night or two later.

"Stay in town all summer!" cried papa in sarcastic glee. "It would be un-American; a family must split up nowadays, separate,—husband from wife; daughters must go visiting about among other families; sons must push out alone into the fishing-camps of Canada; it's the correct thing. Isn't a long winter-time enough for those 'whom God has joined together' to endure one another? And even in winter must not the wife depart for Florida or Virginia?"

"A man and wife ought never, except under the gravest necessity, be separated," said Jack, carving the turkey solemnly. It was one of his finest truisms.

"Ah, Jack!" cried Florence, gladly echoing him, and nodding at the same time to mamma. Jack seemed to speak from the heart.

As the season advanced there was every indication of its being very gay. Florence returned to the city, felt the bracing October air with increasing health and strength. She realized that she had given her husband a year of invalidism, and she determined to make amends. She planned many dinners. She determined to have a ball in Christmas week. Thanksgiving Day they dined their college foot-ball team—crestfallen with its defeat by Yale—and gave them a reassuring dance afterward, the wide drawing-room being elaborately done in crimson for the occasion. They held two grand receptions. They entertained celebrities. Papa became a great talker; he had shrewd, keen, level-headed ideas of things in spite of his amusing pessimism; it being once admitted that we were the worst-managed, most ill-administered government in the world, he acknowledged we were doing very well. Grant him the fact that the city was managed by a den of thieves, and it was a capital place to live. He loved dearly to growl, but he never cared personally to participate in an effort of reform. He had the usual New York business man's penny-wise and pound-foolish attitude. He never could leave his business long enough to more than vote, and "this complicated, new-fangled system of registration and voting in vogue was beginning to take a great quantity of time, don't you know," even for that!

One night—it was in the middle of February, and many things were crowding in before Lent—they had been to a dance and cotillion at a large fashionable house on North Washington Square. Florence, as was her wont, went first, before removing her wraps, to the baby's crib. She stooped and leaned over. Dorothy was flushed and feverish. Her little blue eyes were wide open, yet she was not making a sound. She seemed to enjoy the vision of her beautiful mamma as she knelt at her crib-side, in her soft fur-lined opera cloak falling half-down her lovely shoulders. She liked to see the glittering diamonds in her ears, in the necklace at her throat, for she laughed and gurgled. Then she began to cough a little.

"Jack, come here!" called Florence.

He was smoking a cigarette just before going to bed. He laid it down on the mantel and crossed the room.

"It's the grip! See how feverish she is! It may be scarlet fever."

"Oh, ridiculous!"

He raised the little mite of human life in his arms and brought it to the light. Florence clasped her hands tragically.

"This comes of my going out night after night, and neglecting her. Oh, Jack—if she should die!"

"It's nothing. She has a cold," he said.

But the next morning Dorothy was worse.

They sent post-haste for Dr. Chesney, and in two or three days the fever was gone, the little throat was better. Florence sat up two nights with the child, while her husband slept. She grew pale with worriment and watching. At the end of a week, Dr. Chesney said gravely: "I must send you at once to Florida—both you and the baby." Dr. Chesney was a finished, polished, skilful little man, with a bald shiny crown. He had a way of ordering people to Florida as he would order them to take a walk or ride. He never especially recommended the hotel in which he had an interest. People found out for themselves which his hotel was, and went to it for the especial treatment. In winter he prescribed Florida, in summer the Adirondacks. As he had recently bought a tract in Ontario, where he was putting up a large hotel, he was already beginning to speak of the " ozone of the Canadian forests." This little doctor, the arbiter of fate of many families, never hesitated a moment to split them up—divide husband and wife; he cared not an atom, apparently, for their moral well-being. He had effected some remarkable physical cures. And one thing can be said of the intelligent little man—he often sent some poor patient to his Southern hotel free of expense. When he did these generous things all the world knew it and liked him for it, and he prescribed for them as a consequence.

"It's for Dorothy's sake *only*, Jack," said Florence, distressed.

"Why, of course you must go," he insisted, half-attentively, for he was perusing the paper. "You must go at once."

How good Jack was! Papa openly protested. "Of course Florence must have her mother with her. Their family-life was to be completely broken up, then. I don't believe it's necessary," he said; "Dr. Chesney is always sending people to his hotels. I don't believe in sitting about and watching every turn of the thermometer. 'Our climate so trying?' Why, it's not so! It used to be severe, but it's changed; it's the finest climate in the world to-day. There is no place that has so much sunshine, so many fine days as New York. If they go to Florida it will be warm and moist, and if they get rid of the grip they'll catch malaria in place of it."

Women, in questions decided for them by their doctor, have a way of ignoring opposition. They talked in low voices now, mother and daughter, of their necessary preparations and of the day they should start, while the old gentleman went on:

"What are Jack and I to do? Don't you owe *us* any allegiance?" It's lonely living in this great house without you. We'll have to take to drink."

Even this threat was unheeded. Jack, in evening-dress, was reading the *Post*, preparatory to going over to his club. It was his whist-night. He had already many times cheerfully advised going to Florida, "if it was best." Florence only thought of Dorothy.

At the moment in his dress-coat pocket was a letter, the writing of which was in the fashionable "long" style. The address nearly covered the entire envelope. Miss Franscioli had written him a business letter from New Orleans. She informed him that she was to be in New York permanently after the following week. She intended buying a "nice little house," and setting up an establishment somewhere. She also planned a small investment in stocks.

It was not worth while to show Florence a business letter. It was not worth while to speak of Miss Franscioli. He had reason to believe his wife disliked her. Why, he couldn't imagine.

XVII.

DURING the days of Florence's absence in the South, Jack saw very little of his father-in-law. The old gentleman did not care very much for his club—had not been brought up to regard it as a necessity. Clubs came into prominence in New York after the war, and his young manhood was passed in antebellum days. Down town he lunched at Parrish's on John Street, and met there most of his old business friends; it was "club" enough for him. He preferred to pass his evenings at home, and very often he went to bed early, having nothing to do. Very often, too, an old friend dropped in, and they sat and talked of the old days and the changes that were going on, and he frequently read aloud Florry's last letter. Mr. Heath loved to revile the modern life and to say all manner of harsh things about it. "This idea of going away South after the first of January," he said, "was mere doctor's rubbish. Can't the women ever stay at home with their husbands and mind their business?" The favorable reports about Dorothy, however, reconciled him a little to his wife's and daughter's absence.

Jack got in the habit of dining at the club. He knew it was dismal enough for his father-in-law at home, but it was a terrible ordeal to have to sit through a long perfunctory dinner and listen to the old gentleman's diatribes, delivered in a most lugubrious, harsh, rasping tone of voice, and levelled at everything Jack particularly affected. They came to see very little of each other, meeting only at breakfast and exchanging news about Dorothy and their wives at St. Augustine.

One morning the old gentleman said: "I think of running down to see them. You'll go, Jack? I'll engage two compartments; it shan't cost you a cent."

"N—no—I can't get away. We have a big 'deal' on."

"To tell the truth, I'm getting lonely," said the elder, as he lit a small cigar.

Jack looked at him half pityingly. "That's just where clubs come in—to lonely husbands."

"I don't believe in it," and the old gentleman beat his fist on the table savagely. "Our family should not be broken up in this way. I admit that Dorothy's health is paramount just now, but should we all go off in so many different directions just because the baby has a sore throat? Family-life is the right life, my boy. Now here is a pretty state of affairs: it's only March, and yet they are in Florida, you at your club—the house is empty. I don't like it. It's wrong; it's abominable!"

"Why, how are we going to help it, sir?" said De Ford amused, standing, legs wide apart, before the low fire of soft coal which was crackling up the chimney. "It's better for the baby, it's better for Florry. Do you remember a year ago? Did you like those days when we went about fearing to breathe while she hung between life and death? I am glad we are able to send them to Florida."

"Yes, and as soon as they do come home we shall have to send them away again, North, to separate for the summer."

"That's the climate's fault."

"The climate! What did Florry's mother do in the old days? At that time people could not procure these temporary divorces so easily."

Jack laughed, and his irate father-in-law went on: "No, no, I'm not talking for fun—I mean it! It's wrong that a man should be left alone among all these city temptations, his wife off enjoying herself somewhere. She is no 'helpmeet' to him. He doesn't protect *her*. Now, Jack, I'm an old city man, and I know the world pretty well, and I hear a good deal of talk here and there. I pick up a good deal. I know what's going on, what with the 'pretty type-writers,' and the 'pretty sales-ladies,' and the working-girl whose head is turned by a little flattery, and who is fond of finery and a new bonnet and cloak."

Jack became very serious. "There is a lot of that sort of thing going on," he said. "It's true, but I don't quite see the connection."

"Why, I'm told it's the married men that do the most of that sort of thing."

Jack nodded. "So I hear," he said; "but I guess if a man is selfish and bad, he is so even if his wife is here with him."

"Not so apt to be. We are poor, erring human critters, Jack. As my good old dominie said last Sunday—I wish you'd been to church instead of driving—we are devilish prone to sin, as the sparks are to fly upward. But if we are left idle, our family-life upset and broken up, how much more likely we are to fall! Take a poor girl and deprive her of family home-life and protection, and she's half-lost already. She has to be devilish strong-headed to keep straight in this vast city. Take a man and deprive him of his wife, his home; send him off to a club, where he meets the very worst sort of characters, as far as women go. Egad! he's got to be strong-headed not to get into the current and go down the stream as the rest do."

Jack acknowledged that everything he said was true.

"This modern American life," he said slowly, "it is strange; it is wrong! There I meet Tom Challinor, Archibald, Harry Talmadge, Disbrow—all married men, with their wives in Europe or somewhere. There is a regular married man's 'set' at the club. I don't pretend to know all that they do."

He did not tell his father-in-law that he had accepted an invitation from Challinor to dine at Delmonico's the Saturday night following, and that there were to be several rather *risqué*, "swagger" young married women present, and at which the champagne and the liqueurs were to be *ad lib.*, and the women were expected to smoke the dainty little Egyptian cigarettes by the dozen.

He put on a solemn face, for it suddenly occurred to him that it was as a philosopher he was examining the question of temporary divorce, and that it was as a philosophic observer of modern life and manners that he would attend Challinor's rather rapid *petit diner* at Del's.

His father-in-law had often spoken against clubs and club-life. This morning, deep in his heart, he acknowledged that all he said was simply true. His father-in-law knew what he was talking about!

He put on his hat and coat and walked downtown meditating upon the dangers and temptations which beset other people in married life. He felt very strong, very secure in himself. He made no personal application of the words he had heard. He was in love with his wife, devoted to Dorothy—*he* was simply adamant. But only the day before a friend had told him that Sundown, the artist, was canoeing it in Florida. The fact irritated him.

"Florry is one of those women who takes a lot of enjoyment in the present," he said to himself. "She likes best the man who is with her. When I think of last summer, I admire my own forbearance; it's because I believe in her, I trust her, I love her."

This little speech to himself, attuned to his own ear so perfectly, gave him a warm pleasant glow, as he marched down Broadway on the left side, with his silk hat so well brushed, his walking-coat with a bachelor's button so *chic*, his stick so light and fashionable. The pretty shop-girls stared and half-furtively smiled; he was handsome as an Apollo. He swung along with a fine air of *aplomb*, of success. He was liked. He was "square," he was ambitious. Nothing so fired his ambition, so poised his flight upward as this walk down Broadway of a sunny winter's morning. The bustle, the noise, the crowd, the roar, filled his heart and nerves like the music of battle. He passed by the towering business houses feeling keenly the motive of the time, of the hour— commerce. He regretted not that the Jews had plastered their names from Grace to Trinity Church, or that the Irish flag floated on the City Hall; he had a fine democratic feeling of "letting the best man win." The grand life of action, of fighting for money and supremacy filled him, surging through his veins like fire. He felt he was a part of the true "great world" of New York, and that the little silly world of fashion uptown was but a puny thing. *Vive l'homme d'affaires!*

XVIII.

WHEN he presented himself at Delmonico's for Challinor's dinner he was still filled with his enthusiasm for business success and power. It seemed to be the all in all for him. He had passed through the youthful love-period—that was over. Women could no longer especially charm him. He would be rich, powerful, a man of business. That very day he had made ten thousand dollars by a fortunate turn; it intoxicated him. A foreigner might think it strange that this man of business cared nothing for his city's political welfare. It was nothing to him. He cared not what Irishman held the reins. Like his father-in-law, Jack occasionally condemned city politics as "corrupt;" but he never thought of giving his attention to the matter. Which of his friends did? Politics in New York, forsooth, were hardly the occupation of a gentleman!

They already asked him to take a responsible position on an important committee of the Stock Exchange—*i.e.*, he was a coming man. Every one knew he was the "brains" of "Beach, Catherly & De Ford." Women played a small part in his future. His wife, to be sure, would always second him finely. He was proud of her beauty. But even his wife—he noticed the same phenomenon the summer previous when she was away so long —did not now often enter into his dreams. She seemed now to be always looking at him, as it were, from the outside, now discriminatingly, and not, as formerly, from the inside, enthusiastically.

Challinor greeted him cordially. He was a pale, modest-looking little man, of the finest manners and the most stoical countenance. He came of most excellent family, and his wife and children were spending the winter on the Riviera.

Archibald, a handsome New York dandy, was a well-known swell, who, in a fit of absent-mindedness, had married a poor but pretty artist. He was a good fellow, and his wife and children were somewhere in Georgia enjoying the pleasant June-like weather. Jack shook him by the hand.

Disbrow, celebrated as a "lady killer," not

at all a handsome man, but a prodigious talker; a nervous, irritable man who had written a series of unsuccessful novels, stood taking off his gloves. He was a well-meaning man among men, and his wife was at present in Sioux City for purposes other than health.

Harry Talmadge—"much-married Harry," they called him at the club. He was a short, fat, exceeding popular man, with a wife who rarely left the city summer or winter while business kept him there. Harry Talmadge had long been an operator on Wall Street, and knew Jack very well. He completed the list of male guests at the dinner. His wife had gone for a temporary stay in the country.

When they entered the little drawing-room out of the dining-room, Jack was surprised to see Miss Franscioli standing before the long cheval glass in a superb Paris gown of black satin. He went up and spoke to her at once. They met now as old *intimes*. Near her stood several handsome women, to whom Challinor introduced him.

Mrs. Bronson, whose husband was forever shooting on the Chesapeake; Mrs. Berrian Deland, who played the part of indulgent chaperon, and complained that her husband was still detained in London on business, beamed on him. Mrs. Bronx, whose husband was spending his time yachting among the West Indian Islands, said to him: "You know I can't endure the water" (here she sighed plaintively), "and my husband is passionately fond of his yacht. What can one do? *Que voilà?* We separate, and I try to worry along without him by means of my many friends."

Mrs. Bronx made an upward movement of the eyelids that was positively saint-like.

Jack took in Miss Franscioli, and was placed next her at table. It was an expensive, elaborate dinner, and there was but one wine from oysters to coffee, after the latest club fad.

"I have been very ill," Miss Franscioli said —"the grip; but I am well again. I have bought a little house here, Mr. De Ford. A new little house, far up on the west side, and it is filled with everything I could find and scrape together in Europe, lots of rare curiosities. Come up and see it."

He had already seen and been in the house, but she said this for effect. She never looked so beautiful to him. The poise of her head, her fluffy, pretty hair, her smile fascinated him. Her shoulders were superb. What style, what *verve* she had! In his then feeling of business conquest he felt he would love to conquer *her*, and trail her, as it were, in his triumphant procession behind his chariot-wheel. They had had several business consultations together, had lunched twice at Savarin's. He felt himself pleased to know of her social success, to learn that she was "positively flooded with the swellest invitations."

Challinor said it was a consolation dinner. Every one present must be deemed in the depths of woe. Then he thought of Miss Franscioli and stammered: "Some of us have escaped——"

She burst out laughing, saying, "You are making matters worse!" And Disbrow quoted, *sotto voce:*

"My heart still hovering round about you,
  I thought I could not live without you;
  But since we've been three months asunder,
  How I lived *with* you is the wonder!"

"Out of sight, out of mind," said Mrs. Bronx, with a laugh, quoting in her turn:

"That friends, however friends they were,
Still deal with things as things occur,
And that, excepting for the blind,
What's out of sight, is out of mind."

Archibald repudiated this sentiment with great vim. Jack remained silent.

Every one else seemed to be pervaded with the idea that marriage was a capital thing to make game of. Wit is fond of her sister, Irreverence. Wit insists on perfect freedom; it admires nothing, it respects nothing. Marriage was but a joke, after all!

The dinner was soon, without losing its decorous character, full of laughter and point. There were several piquant little stories of a worldly turn. American gentlemen are never very "free" in their cups with their women, even with those they do not entirely respect, and the conversation never verged on the "impossible." Challinor had in, at the end of it, the pretty Spanish *danseuse*, then attracting much interest in New York. She was pretty and graceful, and, when she finished her *pas seul*, the men filled her slipper with champagne and drank out of it. It was considered a gallant act. De Ford preferred his in his glass. The room was brilliant with light, the table a mass of roses, the music of the Spanish guitars was soft and sensuous. There was a luxurious air of splendor over all. Archibald, who was an exceedingly proper, if a somewhat dull young man, leaned his elbows on the table— he was smoking a cigarette—and looked across at Jack. Apparently he was having, at the instant, a momentary bad half-minute of self-reproach. "Our poor wives in the South," he said to Jack, "may they soon be well enough to come home again!" and he drank a bumper to them.

"Yes, here's to Dorothy," said Miss Franscioli quickly. "And here's to "Madonna" also, as Mr. Sundown has rightly named Mrs. De Ford."

"My wife writes he is in Florida; she saw him," said Archibald. "Now Sundown is a true artist; he feels. I always wished I'd studied art, don't you know?"

"Do you think you can *feel?*" asked Miss Franscioli, admiring his smooth, fat aristocratic face with its drooping mustachios.

"Ah, how can you ask me?" And Archibald put on a most adorable smile.

"Oh, you men! You can never understand what it is really to feel!" And Miss Franscioli sighed. Immediately after she lit a cigarette and entered into a pitched battle with Disbrow over Gilbert and Sullivan's operas, which she detested. When they rose from the table Jack sought out Archibald.

"Is Sundown in St. Augustine?"

"I believe he is, at the Alhambra—yes."

"Ah!"

"A d—d handsome fellow, too, De Ford; has a frightful reputation as a lady-killer. Is a good shot, lived four years in Paris, and was always fighting duels at unearthly hours in the morning in the Bois de Boulogne. Oh, I used to know him very well, but I didn't care to have him call; I prefer him at the club."

"Is he so disreputable?"

"Now see here, De Ford, you and I are married men, by God! We look on these things in a different light from most men, of course. We're particular, egad! We both have deuced handsome wives, and they're away alone."

Jack tried to push him away; but Archibald, who was affected by the wine, insisted in a louder voice.

"I—I say, they're both handsome, and of course they're both—strictly—there's nothing they dislike more than flirting, of course. But at the same time they're human, De Ford—old man——"

He could have knocked Archibald down, he was so angry at his stupidity.

Miss Franscioli sought to interfere to lead him away, and it made De Ford only the angrier to have her bestow this mistaken kindness.

"Some men are born idiots," she whispered. "Don't mind what he says."

De Ford was pale and silent. He had not really the slightest cause for anger against poor Archibald, as he had led him on, yet he was dreadfully irritated.

"Ah, *you* can feel," whispered the tall beauty, scrutinizing him narrowly, with a half-smile through her lorgnette.

"Well, I'm not a blockhead, anyway," he said shortly, turning away from her.

He went away soon after this, and returned home in the rain. His own cab had not come for him as ordered, and he did not wait for another to be called. He was too nervous, too feverish. At the house-door he found, to his intense disgust, that he had forgotten his latch-key, and he rang and rang in the pouring rain, waiting for a servant to open the richly decorated door. Presently he heard a rattling of chains and saw a light. The door opened slowly, and his father-in-law put his head out.

"Oh, it's you, is it? Do you realize what time it is? It's nearly two."

The old gentleman never looked so grotesquely cross, so ludicrously peevish. Jack's good-humor returned.

"Then it's high time you were in bed, sir," he laughed.

Mr. Heath looked at him furiously, but said nothing.

"Poor papa!" Jack continued. "Life is not half so pleasant now without them, is it?"

Papa softened a little. "Why, the house is like a graveyard," he replied, and went back upstairs in his dressing-gown, looking very much like old Gargantua himself.

XIX.

THE representatives of the old New York life and the new life, the home-loving gentleman of a past day, and the young man of the present, who must needs be somewhat in the fashion, and who merely used the old house in Gramercy Park for his brief lodgment, saw little of one another now for some time. Mr. Heath went South to find a home, if he could, in a sultry hotel-parlor or the dull discomfort of his wife's hotel bedroom. He was not silent in the midst of his misfortunes. He protested against the horrible publicity of hotels and the stupidity of colored waiters, the need of being agreeable to a horde of strangers, the elevators, and the numberless children who tumbled against one and drove so recklessly into one's legs and corporation. He had travelled in Florida before, and they had nothing new to show him now but their "palatial" hotels. He was soon tired of the "splendor" of these affairs, of the crowd and the music, and the continual feeling that he must be at Saratoga on a muggy day in August! After two weeks of it he fell into a settled melancholy and pleaded for a speedy return North. Dr. Chesney had run down for a few days, and as Florence was still rather languid from the warm dulness of the weather, he advocated their going on to his hotel in the Pines farther south.

"There is a very comfortable watering-place on a pretty bit of green, with some capital trees," said Mr. Heath grimly. "It is located in a spot they call Gramercy Park. There are very comfortable beds there, and one gets capital coffee and the morning papers as soon as he's up. It is also called Home. Do these well-dressed people we see careering about here know what such a place is?" Mrs. Heath, who secretly sided with him, said nothing.

"I want to go home, papa, quite as much as you do," said Florence, who had been holding the plump little Dorothy on her knee. "Indeed, indeed, papa, if it were not for baby I would not wish to stay away from Jack a minute. But what does Dr. Chesney say: 'That it would be suicidal to go to New York for a month yet.' Don't you know how sorry I am for poor Jack, sitting there alone night after night in the great house, thinking of me and of Dorothy? I write to him every day and tell him everything we do. I wanted to tell him about Mr. Sundown's reading to us yesterday, at the old fort; but I kept myself from it, as he's begun Dorothy's portrait, and it's to be a secret. I wish he could leave business and come down here. But he can't, and it's providential that we came, for Dorothy is perfectly well now."

"Well, Jack isn't!" burst out the old gentleman. "That is, he's not happy. He's not himself. He's out at his club till all hours every night, and it's doing him no good."

"Well, I'm very glad he does go to a club," rejoined Florence, resolved to applaud—in public—everything her husband did. "It amuses him. He enjoys billiards and whist. I like to have him go to the City Club, the men are all so swell and so aristocratic. I like to get his letters with the club seal."

Her father held up his hands in protest. "Club seal! He ought never to date or receive a letter except at Gramercy Park! Ah, how balmy and pleasant it must be there now! I can see the tulips springing up in the flower-beds. Spring always gets into the enclosure before it appears anywhere else. The grass was already green before I came away."

"Poor papa!" said Florence with a pitying smile.

Dr. Chesney happened up just then with a telegram in his hand. He looked especially smooth, round, shiny, and well-groomed. "See what you are escaping," he laughed. "A terrible blizzard has set in, thermometer at zero, wires all down, snow three feet in Broadway. Now, do you want to return North? The dispatches say there never was anything like it—not for fifty years! New York is completely snowed under! Trains can't get through. It's something terrible!"

"And Jack!" cried Florence alarmed.

"Now, don't worry about your husband," said the doctor. "He is safely ensconced in that beautiful old house on Gramercy Park. Perhaps for a day he won't get down to business; well, it will do him good. He will have time to write us a long letter, describing this terrible case of weather. Ah, my dear, I'm very glad this little life is not subjected to it;" and the good doctor bent down and kissed the little cooing mite, with a vast show of affection.

Florence turned to her father in triumph. "So this is your mild spring, New York climate, papa, the most 'salubrious' in the world?" she laughed.

The old gentleman for once had nothing to say. Papa, it must be confessed, looked rather put out. When the doctor was out of hearing, however, he said, with a shrug: "It's another of his 'whoppers' to keep people down here, now he's got 'em here. Blizzard or no blizzard, the old house is warm enough with the new patent furnaces; they're sufficient to heat a church. I'd rather be there than here, blizzard or no blizzard. It's sure to affect hides. I'm going North as soon as I can—just as soon as I can."

But they persuaded him two days later to see them comfortably settled at the Pines, before he left them to go North. Sundown had commenced a very charming portrait of little Miss Dorothy, held in the arms of Clarisse, the jolly-faced *nou-nou*. He worked very leisurely at it, claiming that he could only paint for an hour in the morning on Dorothy's account. Florence designed the portrait as a surprise to Jack. For this reason she had suppressed the fact of Sundown's presence in St. Augustine, and had cautioned papa and mamma against making any reference to it. Sundown was especially clever in his young children's portraits.

He painted them in pretty attitudes, caught, as it were, in a momentary swift evanishment. He painted Dorothy pulling apart the petals of a red rose. And if we were inclined to give a Hawthorne-like meaning to Dorothy's act, the red rose might represent in our minds the marriage of the little maid's parents; for was this Southern flight not entirely due to her? And the Northern flights afterward?

XX.

THEY came up from the South to remain only a few weeks at home before it became necessary again to seek out an abiding-place for Dorothy through the period of her second "dangerous" summer. Little by little Florence's life, and the entire family life, began to centre about this remarkable little child, whose dainty curls and chubby fingers meant so much to both generations. Florence proposed a cottage near the sea, where all could be together, and papa and Jack go and come from business every morning and night.

Jack was not averse to this, but he was not especially enthusiastic for the plan. Insensibly he had grown used to separation. The freedom of bohemianism is very attractive to some men; it had its attraction for him. He had met several actors and one or two famous actresses who knew the world, and whose wit and brilliancy amused him.

During the month of May, when the home-life began again, he often came home tired from business and ready to laugh and be amused, and found his wife wearied out by a "headache." There seemed to be no response to his buoyant protestations. Florence, he found, was seldom able or willing to "do" anything. She did not care to go out. He could not persuade her to go to the theatre. The evenings seemed long, and, he was forced to confess, dull, passed in long discourses upon Dorothy, and in telling him what she had seen and done in St. Augustine. But her sweet girlish beauty remained. He still worshipped her, still reverenced her wishes. If he yawned as he sat in the dimly lighted drawing-room as she lay in some soft white dress upon the sofa, he concealed it admirably. She never dreamed he was bored—not by her, but by the dull inaction.

For a week he did not go out in the evening himself. He read aloud from Dickens, from Mark Twain. He wondered why he was so unsatisfied. Had he not had sufficient excitement on 'change all day? The long, solemn home dinner, the long, dim evenings—Florence never liked much light in the room—came to be almost unendurable to him. He longed for something to combat, to conquer, at least to stimulate him.

He contrasted the gay social life at the pretty little jewel-box of Miss Franscioli on Riverside Drive. It was always gay there. The very fact that Florence felt so sure of him annoyed him. Her trust in him was almost too perfect, too implicit. In her sweet presence, a delicate flower, so pure, so good that in his better moments he almost heard seraphic voices singing around her as she lay, her jewelled hand in his—at such times his queer jealousy of Sundown floated out of his mind and disappeared. They never mentioned his name.

It was not *always* dull, and Florence was at times lively enough and like his recollection of her before marriage. But these were occasions when he brought a friend or two in to dine. She thought Disbrow immensely entertaining, and she was sorry for poor Mr. Challinor, whose wife was always away. She brightened up when they were present. She was herself. Why did she not appear as gay and as charming for him alone?

Sometimes he teased her about it. "You never said so many good things in your life,

Florry," he said one evening after his friends had gone, 'as you did to-night. You were like your old self. You laughed and chatted with Disbrow until I began to feel a bit jealous. You were amusing, and those odd stories about the alligator and the negroes——"

"Those I cribbed from Mr. Sundown," she laughed. "He had so many of them. You know we met him at St. Augustine and afterward at the Pines." Jack nodded but said nothing. "Don't you want me to be amusing, Jack?"

"But when we are alone."

"Jack, I love you. It's enough to have you near me. We need not feel we've got to entertain each other, need we? The idea of married people setting out to entertain each other! How ridiculous it would look! Papa calls us a pair of spoons as it is. Isn't love enough, Jack? It's because I'm so contented and so happy that I am satisfied. I want nothing further. What are theatres, dinners, dances, receptions—which I *always* hate, anyway—what are they compared with Dorothy and you? Ah, Jack, I have reached my goal—it is happiness; you may call it—dulness."

He kissed her gently, then he lit a cigar. Yes, it was "happiness."

The next night, after sitting in the semi-darkness with his wife for an hour after dinner, he grew restless and walked to and fro across the wide room. They had been silent for many minutes—he feeling that somehow he was half-unconsciously drawing away from her, and constantly endeavoring to repress his sense of *ennui*. It is true the young man had few resources outside his business. He had come to the time when every day he closed his desk it was with a feeling, "Now my work is over, I can play." He came up town with a vague desire for amusement. Other men he knew were the same. Tom, Dick, and Harry were always telling him of some lark they had been on the night before. He was young, too, and vigorous. He was not averse to a little fun, but this coming home to read aloud, or to sit in the semi-darkness—well, for Florence's sake he would submit and endure a good deal; but it became a dreadful bore.

There came a ring at the electric door-bell and Sundown was announced. Instantly there was a great change in Florence. She sat up, fluttered across to a little oval mirror beneath a gas-jet, turned up the gas, directed the heavy cut-glass chandelier to be lighted.

"Oh, I wish I had put on my pink crêpe gown," she exclaimed vexedly to Jack, "I'm so particular with Mr. Sundown. He notices everything."

Jack pulled at his mustache, watching her, and backing up awkwardly near the mantel as Sundown, in the affected Paris pointed beard, long hair, a lock negligently falling into his eyes over his high forehead, entered.

It is the latest *fad* among some of our swell young artists and *littérateurs* to be mistaken for exiled Parisians.

Florence greeted him warmly; Jack nodded without extending his hand. Immediately they plunged into talk about Florida and Florida people. Jack, without a word, went into the library, where his father-in-law was asleep in his comfortable leathern armchair, and grand-mamma was quietly reading her religious weekly. They heard Florence bubbling over with laughter. "Go in and see Mr. Sundown," said Jack. "I guess I'll run over to the club for a few minutes." Mrs. Heath, much pleased, took off her spectacles, rose, and went into the drawing-room without a word.

"Even she prefers that Paris lackadaisical dandy to me," he said to himself grudgingly. As he went out through the hallway, all three were laughing at one of Sundown's entertaining negro stories he had picked up in the swamps of Florida.

Jack went out into the calm, clear night and saw the moon rising above the trees of the little park. It seemed to him a soft and sensuous May moon, full of a wicked delight —of invitation to a voluptuous flight from everything that was considered particularly respectable. Around the square loomed up in dark outline the uneven line of brown-stone houses. Across the way rose an apartment building striking the starry sky at an enormous height. There were many people passing in the street. There were crude eastside lovers lingering along on the outside of the high iron fence. The fountain was playing in the moonlight. Inside the park were many little family-groups, sitting at ease and secure from intrusion. He was somewhat startled to hear the shrill voice of a boy cry out to those within:

"Say, ye's think 'cause we's can't git in, ye's owns the earth, don't ye's?"

He hailed a passing hansom, lit a cigar, and getting in, directed the driver to go to the City Club. Here he found Challinor, who had been having a rather "heavy" dinner with a few friends invited to meet Lord Sandbury, a young English nobleman who was in New York for the first time.

Challinor grasped his hand and beamed all over. "Just the man we want, De Ford. Wife gone out of town again? Still here? How is it you're out? Ha, ha, old man— been dining, you know—forgive all I say. Now, I've got Lord Sandbury on my hands this evening. He hates theatres, and's after nine, most ten anyway. I've been telling him about the Franscioli, typical *fin du siècle*, eh? We're going up there. She has a *musicale* to-night. Come along with us?"

At first Jack refused. There is nothing so unpleasant usually for a man who hasn't dined and wined to any extent to have to do with men who are somewhat under the "inflooence."

Wine of any kind, even the cheap and harmless California clarets, were rarely seen on Mr. Heath's table. Occasionally with great pomp, on a birthday or a holiday, the butler opened a bottle of champagne. Jack, although he sat at the head of the table and carved, was quite unable to alter this wineless rule. It was the rule of Mr. Heath's youth in New England.

Challinor dragged Jack into the elegant *café* of the club, where round the little tables groups of men were sitting, and ordered another bottle. In the midst of a group who were listening to a rather broad story by Disbrow, he observed a "leggy" blond youth with the faintest suspicion of a mustache. It was Lord Sandbury. He was very handsome, very British, and wore a white vest cut rather high. He had already achieved a reputation in London by figuring in what may be termed a "coming out" divorce scandal. Many young noblemen had made their *début* in that way. It gave them a social *éclat*, as was said.

Jack soon warmed up with the wine and told a good story of his own. He told a story very well, and was already beginning to be in demand. Amid the laughter at the conclusion of his tale Lord Sandbury slapped him on the back, and swore he must run over to London with him and tell that story to H. R. H!

"Come," said Challinor, looking at his watch, "go with us, old man; we will make a night of it!"

Jack thought of Sundown and his pointed beard, and nonchalantly lit a fresh cigar and went with them. Lord Sandbury called him a "thoroughbred." It occurred to him to give a dinner: Lord Sandbury was a great card. Then he thought: "Under the same roof with *her?*" And his vague fancy of a dinner fell into absurdity.

XXI.

THE new little house in Riverside Drive was one of a row of new little houses—very stony staring little houses they were, looking like dry, rocky chasms over which a river formerly used to flow. The stone stoops were universally built out ruggedly into the street and architecturally made much of. Occasionally the stone stoop seemed to be larger than the house itself, to catch the eye first and to prevent the eye from going any farther. Nor did the little houses look particularly habitable. They were too "attractive" to be comfortable, too "rocky" to be lovable, too fussy to become homes. A very "bridey" bride might have moved into one of them, but before very long she would have been willing to move out again, and into a plainer, more domestic-looking house. The groom, were he a man, would soon grow tired of rocky and bricky gingerbread-work, and consign the smart contractor who built miles of these enormities, and the smart dealer who sold him one at an exorbitant price, to everlasting perdition.

It was before one of these rocky affairs, No. 2871, that their carriage stopped that gorgeous May night, with the full luxurious moon pouring its white light upon the irregular façade, and shining from the plate-glass windows. There were one or two other carriages standing opposite in the shadow, and they heard music coming out of the half-open windows.

They mounted the winding stoop. They pressed a button and waited.

"Er—er—a typical New York modern house, Lord Sandbury," said Challinor, pointing to the façade with his cane.

"And very dangerous, I'm sure."

"How so?"

"Why, for children; if I was a lad, don't you know, I wouldn't be quiet without climbing up that granite front, don't y' know?"

They laughed. "What'll he say to the typical woman inside?" said Challinor.

"Is she also of this extraordinary stony character?" asked his lordship.

"Yes, adamant," said Jack quietly.

Presently the door was opened by a tall beautiful woman whose face was full of color and whose eyes flashed in the moonlight. It was Miss Franscioli herself.

"Oh, so glad to see you—Mr. De Ford—of all men—and Mr. Challinor!"

"Lord Sandbury," said Challinor gravely, "the last importation."

Lord Sandbury bowed: "Another American custom, I presume?"

"For a hostess to receive her guests on the door-step? Yes," interposed Miss Franscioli quickly. "Especially as we have such a gorgeous front-stoop. Yes, Lord Sandbury. But I'll tell you something dreadful has happened in my household, Mr. De Ford." She seemed to add his name as if he were responsible for it.

"What is it?"

"A strike. My butler and all my servants have suddenly up and left me. Did you ever hear of such a thing?"

"Perfectly astounding," said Challinor, amused, "that any one should ever want to leave you!"

Lord Sandbury was much interested. "It's very odd, don't you know," he said, "quite American."

"Yes, it's true too. Come in and let me tell you about it. They knew I was going to have a party. They waited until six o'clock. Wasn't it abominable of them? All except my French maid, who would have struck too—she's fully wicked enough—only she can't speak l'Anglais and couldn't understand a word of what they said. I was at my wit's end, but I sent to Lelanne's, and the house is full of stupid waiters. Thus we shall be taken care of for a few days."

"Very extraordinary!" laughed the Englishman. "Very American!"

They entered the square hall, and found the house in dazzling brilliancy from the many electric lights of different colors.

"They waited till they thought they could do what they wished with me," said the Franscioli, laughing. "The wretches! But luckily I was not alone. I had Miss Brown, and my aunt, Mrs. Stead. Look at my hands; aren't they like beets? They have been up to the elbows in hot dish-water."

She looked very charming as she spoke. She had so much life, such high color. The necklace of pearls she wore showed against her white skin, like clots of country cream on milk.

In the highly decorated, richly furnished drawing-room were a dozen or so people, chiefly of the "smart" set. Mrs. Berrian Deland was fanning herself in a corner and talking languidly with Mrs. Bronx. They all looked astonished to see De Ford enter, and delighted to see Lord Sandbury, whose "story" had preceded him. A Herr Professor Volinski—or Hair Professor, as Challinor called him—was about to play something of Liszt's on the grand piano, which had its top raised to give a louder effect. He was high-priced, and the drawing card of the evening. Miss Franscioli took Lord Sandbury in, in triumph, and presented him to her aunt, Mrs. Stead, Mrs. Deland, and half a dozen ladies in order, paying no attention whatever to the Herr Volinski.

"Lord Sandbury is writing a book on America," she laughed, "and he is here to learn how we put down strikes. I don't suppose he cares two straws for music, but he must be kept quiet and listen." She turned to him and whispered Herr Volinski's outrageous *prix pour deux heures.*

Herr Volinski immediately commenced to bang, and every one in the drawing-room and the library, which opened out of it, relapsed into attitudes of deepest interest, one might almost say, concern. After a half hour had glided away Miss Franscioli went back to De Ford, as he stood in the doorway looking rather bored. "Give me your arm," she said, "and we will go where we can talk, and where we can hear the music quite as well as here."

XXII.

THEY passed through the hall, out on a deep, covered piazza at a tower on the side of the house, lit with many pretty Chinese lanterns. The night was warm. There was a cosey divan covered with rugs, above it a large Japanese umbrella. The next lot was not built upon, and the view was open to the river, which, below the Drive, floated dark beneath the moon, and was dotted here and there with boats and brilliant lights. For New York, the scene was sufficiently romantic.

Miss Franscioli threw herself upon the cushions into a corner of the divan, and De Ford seated himself near her.

"I reserve this for my friends," she said; "I alone may come out here before the music is over. Isn't it quite delicious? Now, tell me why you are here alone?"

He looked confused. "I wish you would not ask me," he said. "You sent our invitation to my office. I did not mention it to Mrs. De Ford—I—forgot it."

"It would have given me the greatest pleasure to have seen her here with you. She is beautiful, and she is sweet and good." She spoke rather coldly.

There was a little silence. Herr Volinski had come to an andante passage, very tender, passionate, and much in keeping with the moonlight outside.

"You can smoke here—it is permitted," she said.

He lit a cigar thoughtfully, listening attentively.

The pink light of the lantern fell upon her oval face and gave it a becoming richness of color. His guilty feeling passed away quickly. The desire to pacify and to please the beautiful woman near him predominated. He would even make love a little; she always seemed to expect it.

"I could tell you why I forgot," he said, "but you would not believe me. I forgot intentionally. I couldn't bring Florence here. You know why. Shall I tell you?"

The music moaned out a passionate, despairing cadence; it was the Moonlight Sonata. Their eyes met.

"I don't think I ought to listen to you, Mr. De Ford." Miss Franscioli put on her demure, young-girl manner. "I think I—I ought to listen to the music."

"You will laugh at my funeral, you will joke over my grave," he said solemnly.

"I will if you put on your tombstone any of those absurd epitaphs I used to discover at Pye:

> "Davy died of eatin' pickles,
> Sammy died of eatin' sickles;
> Both are dead, dear little twins,
> Cut off afore they had no sins!"

"There was one I remember in an old buryin'-ground in Alabama, not that it quite hits off your character," and she laughed.

> "Here lies Rufus, lyin' still,
> For where lyin's not allowed
> Surely Rufus's lyin' still
> Up beyant the golding cloud!"

Herr Volinski had come to his loud fortissimo passages again.

"I *could* tell you," persisted De Ford gloomily, "but I won't."

"I will tell you one thing that is certain: I am sure that Northern men never know how to make love!"

She pronounced her i's deliciously, turning them, in Southern fashion, into ahs.

"How should it be made?"

"This way," and she gazed passionately into his eyes: "Jack—Jack, do you remember the day you stopped my horse in the road? You were coming to Rye. In the carriage behind you were all you held precious in the world, yet you leaped out and risked your life to save mine! Jack, from that day to this, you have never spoken of it and I never have. I never dared. From that day you won me to do with me as you will. I love you! You have my secret. That is why I came to New York to live. O Jack! I love you madly! There, is not that pretty good?"

He rose, trembling, and walked unsteadily to the railing of the wide piazza. "It's true," he muttered; "I wish it were not."

She followed him laughing. "Am I not a fair actress, now? Did I not do that well? Oh, I've been a good deal on the amateur stage in New Orleans."

"Where have you not been, and what have you not done!"

"Everything, everything! The world's a squeezed orange to me, Mr. De Ford—or should one say squoze?"

She looked up into his eyes with a subtle, inquiring glance. She was always amusing to him, and he burst out laughing. Then he said: "At least, you are never in earnest."

"I dare not be."

"You would dare anything!"

"A fine compliment you would pay your hostess!" Her chin went up in the air. "Know, then, that I am one of the most timid of my sex; that most of all I need some strong, *good* person to cling to. I have discovered a truth—a woman cannot stand alone. The war has taught us Southerners some fine facts: it's united we stand."

"It taught you not to struggle for independence."

"But how can the myriad, in-rushing tempests of men be kept at bay? I say it is war always between the man and the woman. There are no half-way measures. It is war— or love," and her eyes fell.

"Yes, Plato, thou reasonest falsely."

The young maidenhood of Louise Franscioli must have been a short, boisterous period, he pondered. Unlike most Northern women, she seemed to spring like a man out of a sensuous, not an icy, innocence.

As they stood by the rail in the moonlight, she whispered: "Must it be war, then?"

He turned abruptly, caught her in his arms, and covered her lips with passionate kisses. She seemed half-bewildered that he had read her aright. She hung her lily head in sudden terror.

"I must never see you again—never—never!" cried Jack huskily.

In a moment he was gone. Thus in him had loyalty won the day! He nobly fled from temptation, and virtue triumphed!

Miss Franscioli, after he had gone, threw herself on the divan and sobbed all the way through a lively little song by a professional soprano, concerning *amour, concours, deplore*. At the end of it she rose, wiped her eyes, then clenched her two pretty hands fiercely.

"He shall come back!" she cried angrily. "He shall grant me the opportunity, at least, to *send* him flying!"

A few moments later Challinor came out where she was sitting beneath the red glow of the lamp.

"Alone?" he exclaimed. "Then may I talk to you? My yacht *Calypso* will be in commission next week. Does your aunt enjoy sailing?"

"Oh, she just dotes on it!" laughed Miss Franscioli, recovered now, and fanning herself leisurely. "But tell me, why did you bring that Englishman here?"

"To marry you," said Challinor unflinchingly. "He's after an American girl. He's rich, too."

She rose and walked into the house. "I'll take another look at him, then!" she laughed. "For I am feeling very poor just now, in purse, in feeling—everything!"

"I wonder where my other friend I brought here is?" said Challinor, looking around vaguely as they entered the house. "He seems to have vanished——"

"Mr. De Ford has a magnificent conscience," she laughed. "He has gone to consult it!"

XXIII.

DE FORD, to do him justice, tried very hard the week following to prevent Dr. Chesney from carrying off Florence and the baby into the wilds of the Adirondacks for the summer. But it seemed that Dorothy's throat could not endure the salt air of the sea. The fact once being admitted, there was no place where they could receive so much attention and care as in Dr. Chesney's comfortable hotel on Moon Lake. Dorothy began to sneeze the first week in June. They left, Jack accompanying them, for the North, three days after the sad event of the first sneeze.

They dismissed the servants from the house in Gramercy Park, and installed a care-taker's family—a queer, hopeless couple, with a crippled son, who rarely emerged from the basement into the upper stories, save by way of a gentle aroma of onions, or a suspicion of rank tobacco-smoke. The old house was closed—the front door boarded up, except a small opening at the side. The blinds were shut, the shades pulled down. Jack's father-in-law arranged his business for a long absence. He was driven to it, he said, in self-defence. Another summer alone in the deserted mansion in Gramercy Park would drive him into Bloomingdale! It was an odd circumstance that in rummaging for his pistol the first night after his return to the city—the strange noises in the vacant house gave him some uneasiness—De Ford found the card which Florence had always treasured, the card which announced to the old couple in the Senegambia that they would always live together. He took it out and looked at it with a smile of sardonic gravity, and read:

Mr. & Mrs. Schermerhorn De Ford,

At Home,

Every Day in the Week
FOREVER!   *No. — Gramercy Park.*

"Forever!" he repeated slowly, twisting the card in his fingers and throwing it back in the drawer. He walked to the open window, and looked out over the trees of the park. Everything was silent; not even a belated cab rattled in the stony street. He had an intense spasm of loneliness; even the crusty old gentleman and the servants were gone now. He thought next day he would try living in one of the noisy little upper rooms at the club which they let out for transients at exorbitant figures. He slept there two nights, and that was all he was able to endure in the close, hot, little chamber. At least, he could have the whole floor to himself in his own house, with the windows open, and a cool breeze blowing through from across the park. The heat had come on to stay, and he was very glad of the cool rooms and the cold shower-bath night and morning. He had promised to remain in the house and look after things, and he felt a little more comfortable even in his loneliness in doing so. He had a sense of virtuous reaction. He immersed himself now in business, running out of town for Sunday to some friend's cottage. After all, it was the old bachelor life over again—only pleasanter. He recalled the days of his boarding-house existence, when he sweltered through two torrid summers in an attic-hall bedroom in Thirty-sixth Street. Life was very hard then—after his father's failure and death. But he recalled that he was very hopeful then, and now all his hopes were realized. Was he any the happier? He was rich; he had married a beautiful, dutiful girl, he was the father of the dearest baby in the world—yet—yet—

Occasionally he stopped on the way downstairs and out in the morning and glanced at Florence's portrait. The face was so pure, so calm, so noble! Did he deserve that sweet girl's love? How had he behaved that night in May, on Riverside Drive? The fire of that stolen kiss still burned on his lips. Something whispered to him that he would never, were he *her* husband, have to separate a day from *her* side. Would *she* consider the daughter before the husband? Would he go home to her, to silence, to dim light, and—stupidity? He realized that life with Louise Franscioli would not all be smooth sailing. There would be terrible rows, but the rows themselves would excite him, stimulate him. He would glory in subduing her or in being conquered by her.

But all that was over now. He had transferred her affairs to another banker, after having the satisfaction of increasing her account to a good figure. He wrote her a kind note, confessing much of his weakness and asking her forgiveness. This he afterward cautiously destroyed. He got Challinor, who was a good fellow, to see her and tell her that all, even distant friendship, must be considered at an end between them. De Ford was a man of the world, and he knew well enough that the affair must either end then or it must end in disaster. Challinor respected his feelings and pitied him. He was not one of those who have much patience with the doctrine that a husband and a wife stand on an equal footing in such matters. It was not a doctrine that was openly scouted at the club. It was only tolerated, when advanced, with amused smiles. The very young married men, who were stranded in town for the summer without their wives, adopted it; but as the years went on all the rich married set very often bought diamonds and silver-ware at Tiffany's, which never appeared afterward to adorn the home circle, or the dinner-table. Challinor bought Rhine-stones. Some men were not even as generous as that!

XXIV.

THE lonely days went on, and the dreary, unremitting heat of August descended upon the avenues and the cross streets, making life unendurable. With the heat and the general desertion of the city by the better class of its inhabitants, a strange, uncouth, vulgar set of people seemed to take possession of things. The real "lady" disappeared. In her place came a loud, over-dressed creature, who seemed to be possessed of only one idea —effrontery. In the elevated trains, the horse-cars, the theatres, this creature—not necessarily the *demi-mondaine*—was omnipresent. Her jewelry was extremely prominent and prevalent. She it was who applauded the great "Buck," a base-ball divinity, as he "slid to second" in the ball-game with the Chicagos. She was on every Coney Island boat with her "lady friend." She dominated the bathing-beaches; she was always on the move. She never minded the heat. She chewed gum in public. If ever addressed by accident, she was very apt to draw back with a loud hiss and a "Sir!" which made the unlucky male wither under her outraged scorn. On the whole, the extreme virtue of this creature seemed to be always over-prominent, and to be carried as it were upon her sleeve for daws to peck at.

He did not allow his nerves to be half so much upset by the enormous activity of the evening newspapers, with their racing editions, and their base-ball editions, and their 'extrys' bawled by multitudinous boys; but the feeling as he went up and down town in the crowded elevated trains, that only the vulgar herd were left with him to toil in town, was hardly an agreeable one. At the club there were men enough. It was crowded, except Saturday and Sunday. There was a good deal of quiet gambling, contrary to club rules, and a good many men came up to town for it. There was a great deal of quiet drinking, too. Fat men and thin men, old and young men, sat, smoked, fanned themselves, and drank enormous numbers of Remsen "coolers," getting up the courage, presumably, to roll home in a cab, and let themselves into dark, gloomy, deserted houses, which they called their "homes."

"Ah, men must work that their women may play," said Harry Talmadge one night at the club. "We are all sweltering here on 'Change every day, and our wives are having a pleasant summer of it. Should they be here at work, too—or should we not work so hard or so long, and go out into the country and be with them? It's a difficult problem to solve off-hand. I have just spent a week at Narragansett Pier with my wife. It amused us to see that pretty Mrs. Breezey kiss her husband with so much abandon the Saturday night he arrived. The little wretch had been flirting outrageously with Lord Sandbury, who was there on a yacht all the week. Breezey is a sober, hard-working lawyer, very conscientious, and very devoted to his pretty wife. He was sweating and grinding at his desk all those hot days. What was she doing? He wrote her every day from Nassau Street; she wrote him just once. Thank the Lord! all wives are not like Mrs. Breezey—eh, De Ford?"

"Which lord?" queried Disbrow in a dry tone.

To keep up appearances, De Ford said, with an air of interest, ignoring Disbrow, "No, indeed!" Generally Jack paid no attention to what was said about wives. Florence was a very faithful correspondent; her letters generally gave a monotonous and strictly accurate account of what was done on Moon Lake every day from breakfast to bedtime. There were always little commissions, numbered 1, 2, 3, etc., for him to attend to, which he turned over to the office-boy to execute. They were not, somehow, letters which he opened with any wild avidity. He knew what they contained. Dorothy was learning to talk. She had now got beyond "ga ga" and "goo goo." This was interesting enough. But from what appeared in this correspondence, life at Moon Lake was extraordinarily monotonous. Florence quoted to him a great deal that a certain Mrs. Mitchell said, who, it seemed, lived near them, on Twenty-second Street. She had struck up an intimacy with this Mrs. Mitchell, who appeared to be one of the wise, religious, motherly sort of persons, for whom he had an especial aversion. Florence wrote that she was a 'pillar' of St. Pancras' Church in Eighteenth Street. He really could not complain of the letters, but sometimes he felt he would like to resent Mrs. Mitchell's oft-quoted advice. He mildly expostulated once or twice, but the cold tone of Florry's subsequent letters caused him to hesitate. Women of the Mrs. De Ford kind—the simple, good wives, who were "sure" of their husbands—have little perspective, and sometimes "bank" too strongly, as it were, upon simple-mindedness in their worser halves. The story of poor Breezey getting only one letter from his wife at Narragansett half lost its point for De Ford. So runs the world. What we have too surely we despise. What we have not we strive for. What we achieve appears entirely insignificant. The French say that marriage is a long, hard highway, without a turning. At the end of the road is a simple, chaste tomb, surrounded by respectable weeping-willows. One sees this respectable finale painfully clear from the beginning of the dual journey. There are no episodes; there are no halts by the wayside—to halt is not respectable! It is plain sailing. Is it not an enjoyable prospect? What! you doubt it? My dear sir, *you* are not respectable!

De Ford left the club for "home" early

that night. As he was going out Challinor, wearing a yachting-cap, entered.

"Oh, I say, the very man I'm after!" he laughed. "It is Thursday. To-morrow afternoon we leave Larchmont for Newport, arriving there next Tuesday. It only means one full business day, Jack—that is, Monday—and we want you."

"I wrote the Catherlys I would spend Sunday with them——"

"Do you wish to bore yourself to death? We are going to have Disbrow, Mrs. Bronx, Miss——I won't tell you."

He knew well enough.

"There will be a full moon. If you like the boat, I'll sell her. You know the *Calypso?* So it will be a 'business' trip!"

"Challinor, I have turned my back on the Franscioli forever, as you know."

"Do you fear her? She is said to be engaged to Lord Sandbury, who is now at Newport—every one says so. She is quiet and sad enough of late, at all events. She hardly ever smiles; she is pensive. It is an opportunity for you to show your goodness of heart."

De Ford was firm, however. It really would not do. He did not fear for himself.

Like the average American that he was, he had the utmost trust in his own integrity. He believed in himself. Young man that he was—not twenty-seven—he had the "worldly" innocence. He thought he had sown his wild-oats when he lived at Cambridge in the "fast set." He relied a good deal on that worldly adage, an adage which time may show to be more universal than was suspected. For why should there be "sex" in proverbs? And why should not a gay girl sow her wild-oats and ever after be good? The theory of the repentant sinner is Christian; the wild-oats theory pagan enough, but the pagans knew human life pretty well.

De Ford had, besides, ambition, and the Franscioli could not help him. She would delay him. He would sacrifice a good deal for "success." A respect for marital vows still won credit on the street. It helped to procure loans; it oiled the wheels of speculation for steady men, and assisted in strengthening the great idea of trust.

XXV.

THE next morning at the office he found that Catherly's wife had suddenly been taken ill, and that his visit there would have to be given up. He would, then, be obliged to pass another lonely and miserable Sunday at the club, looking over the daily illustrated papers? Rather than that he had about made up his mind to run down to Long Branch, and put up with the Jews, infidels, and Turks of the large caravansaries at that resort, when Challinor came into the office and renewed his invitation.

"You must give up that visit to old Catherly's. We want you, Jack. You need have little to do with the Franscioli. I intend to devote myself to that pretty baggage——"

"Oh, no," said Jack, "it would be impossible, quite——"

But Catherly happened in just then, and Challinor appealed to him. "Why, it dovetails in perfectly!" said the former in his hearty manner. "Go, Jack, by all means. The market's dull; you can stay a week. My wife will be all right by next Sunday, and we'll expect you then. Go, my boy, and have a little out-door fun. You're too serious of late. Mr. Challinor, introduce him to a few pretty girls and get him to flirt. He used to be a good hand at that sort of thing. Jack, go along and have a good time and flirt!"

"Yes, but I fancy it's just that sort of thing he's most afraid of," said Challinor dryly.

"Afraid? He? Why, he's getting to be an old maid! Take him with you, Challinor, and set some of your pretty widows after him. Ha, ha! Stir him up! He's too much married. If he talks stocks, throw him overboard. Let him frivol—gad! He was a gay boy once. He could drink us all under the table, but now—bah! He's too staid—too much married—and he's getting to think he's a coming 'Little Wizard.' Off with you both, boys, and have a good time!"

The good-natured, jolly Catherly almost pushed them out of the door in his eagerness.

De Ford yielded at last to Challinor's importunity. They went out and had a pleasant little lunch together at Del's, on Beaver Street, and the pint of champagne *frappé* helped to quiet his conscience very well. When Challinor left him, he promised to meet them at Larchmont, where the *Calypso* lay at anchor, that afternoon.

He ran up town to pack his valise, and the old Gramercy Park house seemed to him actually to frown with dismal prophecy. A ray of light fell across Florence's portrait, and he could see her counterfeit presentment, her face so pure and noble, from the stairs as he mounted them. He paused a moment.

"It is as if Florence were dead!" he said aloud, realizing sadly that the old, perfect, intertwined life and love had departed. He found a flask containing brandy in his room, and took a long pull at it. "Hang it!" he said, "as Catherly says, I'm getting to be an old maid! I never wanted to come here into this great house. It's never seemed quite like home to me. I wish, I wish Florry and I were poor as church-mice, but living, happy and always together, in a cheap Harlem flat! Married! It's a joke! I hardly see as much of my wife as Sundown does!"

He was delayed in finding his flannels and his yachting-shirts. Everything vexed him. He missed the right train, and when he arrived at Larchmont he had to persuade a small boy to row him out to the *Calypso*, which he saw was rapidly weighing anchor, preparatory to starting. When he reached the yacht, he found they had almost departed without him. As the struggling small boy rowed him alongside, Challinor called out to him:

"We almost gave you up. Miss Franscioli persuaded us to wait five minutes longer. If it were not for her, we would have taken advantage of this western breeze and started eastward. We would have left word we would pick you up at New London."

Miss Franscioli leaned over the gunwale, bowing and smiling serenely. She was in a charming white yachting-suit, her cap trimmed with gold lace. Challinor stood behind her, in comfortable white flannels. Disbrow was sitting in a wicker-chair, talking with Mrs. Bronx. There was an elderly lady, dressed in black—Miss Franscioli's aunt—in the background, who was known as Mrs. Stead.

The yacht was large and roomy, being built for comfort rather than speed. Jack quickly mounted the companionway. Miss Franscioli gave him her hand. He felt a strange joy in reading her eyes again. She had not changed. It was almost as if an interval of months had not elapsed since the night of the *musicale* on Riverside Drive.

"I knew you would come back to me," said her dark, welcoming eyes, full upon his. But there was, too, a fine innocence in them, he thought.

There followed dreamy, cloudless days, in which for the first time in his life De Ford felt himself grappled in the secret, passionate love of a reckless woman "who dares." It was new to him to be courted in this way. He felt its subtle power. It was not over-delicate, over-refined; but it was powerful and genuine. It was not the calm, peaceful love of his wife condensed into a sudden excess; it was a new, wild, absorbing passion of the soul. He felt himself nearing the brink of the precipice, and drew back and hesitated. There were kisses lingering on her ripe lips for him; there were languid, soft glances which told him much. After a day or so, her feeling was almost undisguised; it was like an open engagement. Every one smiled; but no one, even the silent quondam aunt, made any objection to this innocent pastime of devotion. Finally, they were always getting into quiet corners by themselves. He read to her Dickens and Mark Twain, as he had done to his wife. Did this bore him? He did not think of the books. Her hand, warm and soft, lay in his beneath the shawls. . . . Presently he began to be lost, as well, in the bewildering passion she developed in him. He sailed smilingly down the stream with her. He could resist no longer. He loved her. . . .

Challinor used to sit and coolly observe them over his cigar for half a hour at a time, as they sat laughing and chatting beneath her white sun-umbrella, on the deck by themselves. It amused this young man of the world to see his friend Hercules playing with Omphale. "Half the fun of the trip would be gone without De Ford," he kept saying, enigmatically, the afternoon of their start.

"Yes," said Disbrow, "I think she will capture him, unless her own sincerity will make her aim less sure. She is a madcap; passion her element. Bah! if all young women were like her there'd be no business done. Men must have less love and more peace and comfort at home than she would grant. What is her place?"

Challinor replied: "Our civilization, with all its devotion to home life, leaves a poor, mean, little niche for her and her passion. They call it 'wicked,' I believe, because it is not meant for home consumption."

"But is not our home-life largely coming to an untimely end? A new club is formed every day. Men are never at home now. Women are always away somewhere 'recuperating.' I say our home-life is over. Rightly, because it is narrowing, depressing, unprofitable——"

"Yes, yes," said Challinor. "It affords a poor sort of happiness made out of dulness. We want something better. We are crazy for excitement, in this *fin du siècle*."

"True, we live at white heat. That is, *more* of us do. It is more universal than formerly. Our 'best citizens' now attend the wicked French ball and the 'Arion' each year. Our churches are filled with penitent women. All our old theological lines are being broken down. To me it is delightful to live in the midst of this upheaval. I joy in it, I participate in it. For one thing, there is an end of the thraldom of marriage!"

Both laughed. Challinor, at the thought of Mrs. Disbrow at Sioux City; Disbrow, at the thought that Challinor would soon have to follow suit.

"There are two separate courses in the menu, or rather two dishes in one course—marriage and *liaison*," drawled Challinor. "But of course the old marriage dish is best for the State. But hang the State! That's what we are saying now. We are after the individual happiness. Just a hundred years ago it was the opposite. We cared nothing then for the individual, but only for the State and we invented a fine one, which we think we are going to stick to until 2000! I make a guess, myself, that we will let the State go and help along rather the individual freedom. So a woman shall no longer need the protection and the confinement of a home. 'Home' will be 'all abroad.' I see it in our city-life."

Mrs. Bronson, who sat near at hand, whispered, leaning forward and looking at De Ford and Miss Franscioli, who were seated in low chairs on the deck near the foremast:

"Look at them! They are positively spooning! There is home-life for you!" And they all laughed.

They were accustomed to bathe every day off the yacht—those who could swim. Miss Franscioli had a "stunning" bathing-suit, and she never could persuade herself to miss her daily dives overboard at rising and again at noon.

One day the *Calypso* was becalmed in the midst of the Sound. She hardly seemed to move. Her great white sails flapped idly to and fro, and the time seemed ripe for a plunge.

Miss Franscioli disappeared in her cabin, and reappeared in due time, having a white bath-robe about her "stunning" bathing-dress. Only De Ford followed suit, and presently the mermaid was swimming with the merman far in their wake.

"See!" said Mrs. Bronson, "how they want to be alone and get as far as possible from the rest of us even in the water!"

But a little breeze rippled across the placid blue water.

"Drop a boat there!" ordered Challinor hurriedly. "Quick, men! This air is carrying the yacht ahead fast." It was some time before the boat was lowered, and the swimmers observed the yacht calmly sailing off, apparently without the slightest regard for them.

Jack began to grow very tired. He turned on his back to float. He was not a great swimmer. The over-exertion had tired him out. Miss Franscioli was fully able to swim ahead and catch the yacht. Jack looked so pale and fagged that she saw he was unable to make much further effort.

"Put your hand on my shoulder," she said. "Keep cool, Jack." It was the first time she had directly called him Jack. "Can't you trust me? Put your hand on my shoulder. There—that's it! Now they are sending a boat!" she said encouragingly.

"I'm tired out," Jack spluttered and gasped.

Then his hand slipped from her shoulder, and he quietly slipped out of sight beneath the waves.

Miss Franscioli raised her hand and shouted "Help, help!" and dived for him.

The boat was now coming fast. A sailor leaped into the water, swift as a bird in flight.

Challinor, observing them from the stern of the *Calypso* with his opera-glass, cried: "By Jove, he's gone under! And—by Heaven—she's dived after him!"

"Depend upon it, she will never let go of him, wherever they are!" And Mrs. Bronson, who did not at all realize the danger of the situation, gave a little laugh.

Mrs. Stead was below, asleep in the cabin. It is probable she would have laughed also had she been there. It was all so very amusing. But Challinor's face was a picture of intensest agony. Had that mermaid twined her arms about him also? He tore off his coat, and prepared to leap overboard off the stern of the yacht.

XXVI.

SHE had saved his life. He was hers now. She could do with him as she pleased.

He had whispered these words to her as he lay in the cabin propped up on pillows that afternoon, and Louise Franscioli sat near him on a pile of the thick rugs of the floor.

"If I had not caught you and you had risen, I meant to clasp my arms about you and go down, down forever into those sunless, awful depths." She said this lightly, as if it were nothing.

"You will have found that it was better—that," he said languidly, "better for both——"

"Drowning is an easy death; I don't fear it. I was thinking not of myself nor of you, but of 'La Madonna.'"

"Ah, yes, so was I," he said half-apologetically.

Challinor came down into the cabin.

"It's a dangerous thing," he said, "to dive off a yacht that is not anchored. A friend of mine—Colby—was drowned that way. A puff of wind comes, and you can't catch the yacht again. You were lucky, Jack, and if Miss Franscioli had not kept you afloat——"

De Ford, who was still sick and weak with the salt water he had swallowed, nodded his head and said nothing.

"This comes of modern athletics for our girls," laughed Challinor. "Bravo! bravo! You shall be presented with a medal of the American Life-Saving Society as soon as we reach Newport!"

"I shall make you carry out that statement," she laughed. "At Newport you say you are also to present me with Lord Sandbury? Perhaps he will yield when he sees the medal!"

Challinor was disposed to tease a little. "Pray, now having saved him, what did you save him *for?*" he laughed.

"To send him at once to his wife and child, wherever they are," said Miss Franscioli decisively. She spoke as if she were the young man's guardian. She sat, her long hair, still wet, hanging down her back, her hands clasped about one knee, in school-girl fashion. Challinor thought he had never seen so much soul, so much disinterestedness in her face before. Odd man! He had been long in love with her himself. Who could save and help himself with such a beauty? She was a siren to sing and draw men on the shoals and rocks, to ensnare men's unwary hearts; always so gay, when he knew her heart was in the depths; free with the freedom of youth, looking always out of her beautiful eyes for sympathy, and getting so often only a gross form of love, of adoration, from men. He knew her to be good, but careless of her reputation as the wind. Had she been poor she would have been a great actress—a second Adelaide Neilson. But now she had too little incentive in life, and no self-direction; she was drifting. She knew and did too much. She covered too much ground. She read everything. Challinor mused within himself, and thought how strange it was that she should care to remain long away from her *fin du siècle* Paris which was her true home.

"Is it this stupid, commonplace De Ford, with his manners of a prince and his good-looking mustaches, which holds her?" he asked himself. "That strange affinity!

Ah, why did she select him? It will bring much sorrow to that lovely young madonna of his——"

De Ford did not go to Canada until September; then he took his wife and Dorothy and nurse on the trip down the St. Lawrence to Quebec and Montreal. He never mentioned Miss Franscioli's name, although he wrote her every few days—letters full of rhymes and nonsense, and containing here and there a line of boyish passion. He was kind and dutiful with his wife, for he never questioned his own quiet, sincere love for her and hers for him. She was always the same—always sweet, gentle, fond—never rising to great heights or depths. To be with her gave him calm and peace. His conscience did not prick him. He enjoyed everything they saw with her eyes, placidly, with a mild indifference.

The affair of the Franscioli was such a different book from his book of marriage. Perhaps he never would have turned to it had not the loneliness of his life in town that autumn—Dr. Chesney thought the Lenox air best for Dorothy—driven him in self-defence (his evenings were insupportable), to seeking some amusement, some "relaxation." He was not fond of whist; and whist is a great preventer of mischief for the idle, and a strong support of the conventions. Billiards was warm and monotonous work. He was rather fond of driving, and the Riverside Drive is one of the finest in the world.

When, after their visit at Lenox, they returned to Gramercy Park for the winter, in late November, the change had come. . . Miss Franscioli now sometimes wrote, in her feverish, brilliant, hopeless letters, sent to the club, "My husband—in the sight of God!"

XXVII.

THE remainder of this little story is soon told. It is not pleasant to tell, and Jack De Ford does not figure quite as one would like to have him. But he never was quite the hero. Perhaps he's no better, no worse, than a number of young married club-men in New York to-day. There's a fashion in these things. "Lead us not into temptation" is a true prayer; "Lead us out of temptation" is also a true cry of the soul, and the man who, largely through the loneliness of living, largely through separation from his wife, largely through the nervous overstrain of daily business, which causes him to yearn for continual excitement, falls into sin—the man who finally breaks away from it, and triumphs over it, is at least deserving of some credit.

This New York world of ours at present appears to care little for its home-life. People rent their houses with their furniture in them, and then go to live in another house and use another's furniture. People live in huge flats and hotels, and there ceases to be any privacy. People never stay long in one house or flat. Change, change, restless change is what is going on! Harmonious, tuneful dwellings change to shops and flats! Neighborhoods alter year by year. Our wives go to the country for long periods twice— thrice a year now. When we come "home" we are very apt to dine for months with our families in a good restaurant. We go abroad, wander over Europe, and come back with still greater abhorrence of "settling down." Philadelphia sets us an example of home-life, and we turn up our noses at that staid town and poke fun at its "stupidity."

Our restlessness invades and pervades the country round. The good folk in our smaller cities must needs do as we do, and family separation is the order of the day. We are so full of energy, insistence, excitement. We must enjoy, to the very utmost, everything that life affords. Our young men want to be "in the swim," to be seen at Delmonico's, or at fashionable clubs. It is never their ambition, these dandies, to go into politics, or to succeed in business (their fathers' only ambition), or to have a career. It is rather to be seen and admired by men and women.

Club-life has come to stay, in city and country. A man may not see anything whatever of his family, and yet not be thought odd. Not at home, he's at the club, or at business, or out of town. His wife does all the visiting—the receptions, the dances. She carries his card. If he goes to a watering-place with his family, separation is even there the order of the day. He finds a "Casino" there, where he may betake himself. It is "uxorious" to be devoted to his wife. It's "silly" to be too fond of his pretty daughters, according to them. A manly man is no longer self-respecting if he lingers long with his family. Every one smiles and says it is "old-fashioned." God grant that this old fashion of the peaceful, family-home may not utterly depart from our national life, as it is rapidly doing in our greatest city!

As time went on, De Ford joined many clubs. He rarely remained home now in the evening. At his club he would drink a little, gossip with his friends, then disappear. Miss Franscioli, tiring of the rococo little house on Riverside Drive, came down and took a charming apartment on lower Fifth Avenue. Their *liaison* was still a secret. She kept her place in society. She was a wit; she was wanted. She refused many advantageous offers. Many suspected the reason; but no one knew.

Meanwhile little Dorothy welcomed a little brother "Jack," and the "madonna" denied herself more and more to the world. She pleaded family cares. It was odd that Sundown, who had continued to be very devoted, ceased his visits rather suddenly. Perhaps he had ventured too far, and made an avowal, and the sweet madonna had gently reproved him. Sundown married, and after that he and his wife were frequent guests at Gramercy Park. He used to say at the club that Florence De Ford was the one noblest woman in all the world, and then he would sigh and hint darkly at her husband's conduct. To do her justice, Florence pretended to be in absolute ignorance of Miss Franscioli's existence. She never suspected Jack. She never knew nor cared to hear about men's "dual lives." She still kept her husband's image high as on a pedestal. She loved him *because* he loved her, and the years rolled on in quiet, domestic happiness. It was quite true he loved and appreciated her more than ever.

There were moments when De Ford felt very content. But there were days when his hollow eyes, and the little blue rings beneath his eyes, gave signs that care and anxiety lay heavy on his heart. Through the summer months, when Florence and the children went into the mountains—Mr. Heath had finally determined to build a handsome cottage in Franconia—he felt his load lightened. There was not that dreadful suspecting father-in-law to confront him every day at dinner. Grandpapa was getting older now, and crotchety, and nervous. There seemed to be a standing enmity between Jack and him. They rarely spoke to each other. In private, to his wife, the old gentleman was often very bitter against his son-in-law. He was certain of nothing, but he had heard vague rumors. Men downtown love to gossip at lunch-time quite as much as their wives uptown. "Why did Jack go out every night so? Why was he never at home. And where did he go Sundays?" *He* often said to his riding-club, or his fishing-club down on Long Island, or—"well, he always had a d—d ready excuse!"

Florence did not complain. She was not

the complaining kind. Far better, ye sweet young wives, to find endless fault and have it out with your wayward husbands! You are too delicate with these fellows; you fear to offend. Besides, habit soon gets to be second nature. Florence was not very strong. Dr. Chesney recommended early retiring and long night sleeps. It was natural for Jack to run off to some of his clubs of an evening. It was the thing to do. Florence always had a New York girl's liking to have her husband "in the swim." She might be, as she said laughingly very often, "a back number;" but Jack must go out, must be in all the swellest clubs. In her innocence she suspected no danger for him. She never knew exactly at what hour his *coupé* drove up in the early morning and he let himself in. She never asked. She even upbraided herself for her semi-invalidism. "There is no home-life for poor Jack in the evening," she said, and it was true. "He *has* to go somewhere. The doctor makes me go to bed at nine. So he goes to his club, or the theatre, or he and his friends play whist. I wish I was well and strong—poor, poor Jack!"

But the end came at last; a stroke of lightning out of the clear sky.

XXVIII.

JACK, indeed, had had many remarkable escapes. Once Florence discovered a love-letter, but he swore it was one a friend had given him to laugh at. It was addressed "Dearest Self," and signed "L." He laughed it off, and confessed it was a note his friend had stolen in joke out of Mr. Challinor's pocket—a letter from Challinor's wife. She did not mistrust him; she had not begun!

The beautiful Miss Franscioli had her seasons of despair, of harrowing remorse. Like many women of great feeling, she was moody and impressionable; she was always at the greatest height of happiness or in the depths of woe. She found it really true that a woman to live, to exist, needs, more than a man, the approval of every one—even of her own conscience! The day of her birthday came around, and brought with it many sad reflections. She was alone in the world; her father and mother were dead. She was now twenty-four. Her future was dark and sombre, yet she could not break with De Ford. That would kill her. There would then, she said, be nothing to live for. Yet nearly all their joy now when together came of champagne. She was not herself until they had dined and she had had her "pint." Again and again she had formally dismissed him; they had parted for weeks, and again and again she had passionately called him back. She had moments of *exalté* feeling, when she would rush off to some church and fall on her knees, praying God to forgive her. She would lie awake all night, praying for Jack's beautiful wife and children, and then appear at Savarin's, downtown, at lunch next day, dressed to perfection, send a note for him, and carry him away for a grand frolic.

He often told her that she brought him no good; that she was his evil spirit; that she would be his ruin. And then she would moan and cry on her knees, and swear she would kill herself. It kept him at last in a continual state of agitation, of excitement. He never knew when she would send for him —or, what in secret he most dreaded, when a telegram would come saying she had been found dead of morphine, which she took habitually. The day of her birthday came to this poor, tempest-tossed young woman. It was now two years since they nearly drowned in mid-Sound, and Jack, to make her a little happier, went to a diamond merchant in upper Broadway and bought her a magnificent diamond star. It cost him a pretty penny. At the same time, as if to make amends in his own mind, he bought his wife a hairpin of Etruscan gold. He was in somewhat of a hurry, being invited out to dine, having just left the Franscioli in tears and morbidly protesting that he no longer loved or cared for her; and he was hastening home to dress for dinner. He gave directions to the clerk to have the jewelry sent. He took out two cards, on one of which he scribbled:

For Louise F.

MR. JOHN SCHERMERHORN DE FORD.

"*To the girl I love best in the world.*"

He slipped this in an envelope and gave it to the salesman without directing it. He was going out to a little stag-dinner at the Knickerbocker Club, given to his friends by an apprehensive young man about to marry.

He rejoiced that he had hit upon a plan to make both women happy that night without him.

When he came home late from the dinner he went directly to bed, not caring to disturb his wife, although he saw a light turned low in her room, and thought once, as he stood outside her door, he heard a sob.

The next morning he dressed rather late, and hurried downtown to business without seeing any one of the family.

In the afternoon, he received a curt note from the Franscioli, thanking him for the gold pin—of a kind, she remarked, of which she had "dozens." The joke about calling her his "wife," she remarked, was rather stale.

De Ford jumped to his feet. "Good God!" he exclaimed, "they've sent my wife, then, the diamond star—and the card!"

He paced up and down the length of his office, trying to think what to do. It had all come of his haste and the clerk's stupidity. Had he known of it before he went downtown, he might have in some way explained it satisfactorily to his wife. He was prepared to tell her that in the way of a joke, merely, he had lost a bet to Miss Franscioli of a hairpin against a box of cigars, and that the card received by Florence addressed to "Louise F." was a mistake. It should have been addressed to *her*. Then the sentiment, "To the girl I love best in the world," was perfectly proper. He would admit that he had sent a plain card with the hairpin to Miss Franscioli, but that in his haste he had put the latter's name—"Louise F."—on the card intended for Florence. To be sure Florence would be surprised at receiving such a gorgeous cluster of diamonds out of a mere sudden whim; but he would kiss her, and explain that, by an easy subterfuge. She believed his subterfuges! But Miss Franscioli's note, thanking him for the pin "of which she had dozens," was mailed at eleven A. M. It was now four. Had Florence been to see the jeweler, or had she gone to the Franscioli's apartments? Perhaps it was too late to lie now. Perhaps he had broken the eleventh commandment: Thou shalt not be found out!

He sat down and cursed his luck, and himself for a fool. What an idiotic inspiration it was to try and satisfy his conscience by making the small gift to his wife in reparation for the splendid present to "the girl he loved best in the world!"

He was quick and skilful of trick and fence, and he was soon hurrying up-town, first to the apartment of Louise, in order to formulate some plan of action. He found that she had just gone out, leaving word that she must see him immediately. She had left a note for him, saying:

"Your wife has been here, and has left a magnificent diamond star, from Sparcus'. I don't know what it means. I have run out to Sparcus' to find out. LOUISE."

"The devil!" he exclaimed, and walked restlessly about the exquisitely furnished drawing-room, in which he had passed so many wildly happy hours. He observed a silver tray containing cards—nearly all were from men. Challinor had called very frequently of late. He wondered if he it was who had caused Louise so much disquietude. She had said to him once: "He is willing to divorce himself and marry me—*you* are not!" But he knew that she would really never marry any one, and never felt any particular jealousy on Challinor's account.

He waited half an hour, and Louise did not return. Good Lord! what a mess he had made of it! How would Florence act? It would come to her at last, like lightning out of a clear sky. He worried, thinking it would cause a break-down in her health. Good God! it would kill her! He would lie, perjure himself, swear that Louise Franscioli was nothing to him. There was an exquisite Parian marble statuette of the Venus of the Capitol in a corner. His eye kept falling on it. He would have been glad to hurl it out of the window. The whole female sex seemed horrible to him—the enemies of his wife! He put on his hat restlessly, and took up his stick and went out down the elevator. The boy seemed to smile covertly and to be extra-deferential. Was his disgrace noised abroad already? He walked up Fourteenth Street, through the crowds of shoppers. Ugh! the sex was intolerable! What coarse, ugly faces; what headgear; what monstrosities of dress! He stopped at Sparcus', and he found that *two* ladies had been there making inquiries. He would go home and face the music. It was nearly six o'clock now. He hurried up to Twentieth Street. He mounted the steps of the old Gramercy Park house, for the first time sneakingly, with head down, feeling like a truant school-boy returning to school for a thrashing. The outer door was ominously closed, not against the weather, for it had cleared away and the air had grown cold. He tried his latch-key, but the door was bolted on the inside. He nervously rang the electric bell, and stood looking furtively about, across the little park with its thin covering of snow. He wondered if the neighbors were watching. He was glad there were no houses directly opposite to spy upon him—he was grateful to the little park! Presently the door opened. John the butler cautiously looked out. "I'm sorry, Mr. De Ford," he said, "but the orders is not to admit you."

The insult was so monstrous that it was like a blow in the face. De Ford made a sudden fierce grab at the fellow's collar, but his hand slipped, and the door was closed in his face. He swore and hurried away to the club. Here a letter had come from his father-in-law for him. He tore it open and read:

"No. — GRAMERCY PARK,
  FEBRUARY 16TH, 189—

"SIR:—What has occurred to-day, and is now known to Florence, has been the outcome of what I have known a long time. I know everything. I have said nothing, but now Florence knows all, too. I have laid before her the plain facts, believing it best. She is naturally much crushed and overcome. I take it on myself to say that we do not wish any scandal. I propose taking my wife and daughter abroad at once, first instituting proceedings quietly for divorce. In what you have done I admit there has been a certain respect for public opinion, which I will try and keep up in these legal proceedings. You will please name an address where your effects may be sent at once, quietly and without any publicity.

"I am, sir, regretfully yours,
"S. R. HEATH.
"P. S. New York is not—thank God!—Paris."

He crumpled the letter in his hand. He knew the stern old Puritan well. He could be depended on for a rigorous performance! So Florence would get a divorce? His friends in the club were eyeing him, and he must preserve an outward calm. He had felt such security! His love for Florence had never faltered—he thought he recognized the belief that he loved her in a finer, higher way than ever before. The dross of his nature had been give to Louise. Man had a composite nature: what did this old Puritan, whose yea was yea and nay nay, know of these things? He went into the dining-room and sat down alone, his head falling on his hands. Some men at a table near by were laughing and joking—about him? He hardly knew them. Said one—his old truism: "A man and his wife ought never to be separated for a day." What mockery it seemed!

XXIX.

HIS friends who dined near him at the club noticed his silence, his uneasiness at dinner.

"It's the market," said one: "I hear he has lost a deuced lot of money lately." This was true enough, but it did not affect him. He sat and stared at a dismal portrait of an ex-President for ten minutes, until some one spoke to him. Then he started up with a smothered cry and walked out of the room. He stood on the brink of life, looking over the precipice. Should he go to the beautiful, adorable woman he had so long passionately loved? Somehow, even the drowning of his despair in champagne and pleasure no longer tempted him now.

"How is Mrs. De Ford?" he heard some one say at his elbow. "Won't you tell her, please, that I am coming to her reception tomorrow?"

Was it true that he had been ruthlessly

thrust from the door of his own home? He and his father-in-law had never got on well since that first year. But not to permit him to cross the threshold was positively cruel. He had no idea the old gentleman was so vindictive. He ordered a "pint," and it began to make him feel very angry. He had been too stunned to be angry hitherto. He took another "pint," then had a cab called. He drove at once furiously to Gramercy Park. He rang at the door-bell, and, when the servant opened it, pushed past him fiercely. De Ford was a courageous fellow, and he was now at a high nervous tension. He was deadly pale, his eyes burned like coal; he was very handsome now; he looked like a handsome devil!

"Tell Mrs. De Ford I am waiting to speak with her," he said sharply. The servant cringed before him.

"She's not here, sir."

"Tell Mr. Heath I wish to speak with him——"

The servant noiselessly withdrew. He was standing before his wife's portrait. He glanced at it—fascinated. The face humbled and quieted him. In the sweet holy glance from her madonna-like eyes there was, he thought, forgiveness and peace. He turned to the other side of the room: there on an easel was Sundown's new portrait of Dorothy in the nurse's arms, which the artist had only lately finished and he had not seen. For two years it had been in the artist's studio untouched. It was very prettily done. He walked over to it, studying it critically.

"Divorce!" he said aloud. She would get a divorce! Would she be so cruel to Dorothy? Had *he* been cruel? He had deceived her, but had he ever spoken an unkind word, or done anything unkind except this one great thing? Was the catastrophe to annihilate him then? Who was directing this harsh policy of hostility? Here was his home—he was driven from it. It was his no longer! How beautiful and elegant it seemed!

He seemed to be kept waiting an unconscionable long time. He sat down, took out his letter, and read it clear to the end. "New York is not—thank God!—Paris——" He thought over a number of men who sinned against their wives, he felt, far more deeply than he. "Well, it's getting to be like Paris," he muttered. At that moment his father-in-law came downstairs and entered the room.

The old gentleman's face was set and stern. His Puritan origin showed itself in the hard lines about his grim mouth. He was relentless. De Ford felt that, as for him, he had committed the unpardonable sin.

"Well, what do you want?" asked the elder huskily, as he pushed aside the portière.

"I want to know by whose orders I am shut out from my home," said De Ford hotly, and rising.

"By mine! This is not your home. You have chosen another——"

"That affair is ended," he said, equivocating.

"Our decision is final." Papa compressed his lips firmly.

"But my wife—my children—I have a right to see them!"

"My daughter is ill. She is not here. She has gone to the house of a friend. The children are with her."

"Where are they? At whose house?"

"That I decline to state at present."

De Ford could not help admiring the old gentleman's dignified bearing. It was that of a righteous judge. There was no relenting. He turned to go.

"I beg of you not to see my daughter for the present. The shock has been too great. The affair has nearly killed her. You see, *she didn't know you*——"

"But this—this is cruel."

"The cruelty is only on your side."

"But—this house——"

"My dear sir, it is not a club; and we do not regard matters of this kind here as they are regarded, probably, among your associates. This is a Christian family, sir—an American family—and we are not living in Paris——"

With that the old gentleman turned abruptly and left the room. De Ford stood a moment in the hallway, twirling his hat. "So—so," he muttered, "the end has come——"

As he got into the cab, he directed the driver to go to No. — Fifth Avenue.

Louise Franscioli received him with all the compassionate tenderness of a sister. She saw that his love was dead. She wept in silence a long time.

"The end has not come until you have seen the madonna," she cried. "And she will forgive you! if I never see you—again." Jack bade her good-night shortly after, and went out to a neighboring hotel.

"The end *has* come," he kept saying to himself. He had not dared tell even *her* of the bad state of his affairs in Wall Street. He was a ruined man!

As he sat up through that long night, sleepless, the wistful, sad face of Louise came to him. It seemed to him that she had taken of him a long farewell. Every one was leaving him, then? The end had come.

XXX.

THE end had come to everything! Jack De Ford went to his hotel room that night fully realizing that a chapter, if not the final chapter, in his life was closed. Indeed, for several hours, as he paced to and fro, he had a mind to close it—to make it final. The firm of Beach, Catherly & De Ford would fail next day, and be posted in the Stock Exchange. His divorce would soon be public news, and there would be a column or so in the newspapers with a scare-head: "*Another Good Man Gone Wrong.*" Ah, it was all this eleventh commandment, "Thou shalt not be found out," which he had broken. He felt no sorrow, no repentance, no remorse especially; only, the end had come.

Such men as he need the sharp blows of public contempt, of direct, manifest dislike, to make them feel remorse. The "sin" of loving two women did not present itself. "Was it a sin at all?" he asked himself. It was not in Utah. It was not in Bible times.

It was now, only by convention. He had never ceased loving his wife. He loved her now. He would give up the other "illegal" woman forever to satisfy this convention.

He had a small silver-mounted pistol, which he had carried for some time. It lay on the marble centre-table of his hotel room. There were seven loaded cells in it. He might easily discharge one of them into his brain. The effect of his death on his wife would be to make her regret her course; to cause his father-in-law to lead the remaining years of his life in bitter self-accusation. But he had no heart for it. He was too old for suicide. He had seen too much of the world. He knew that his life had not ended. There was still enough in him to live and cry for "success" and final triumph. He still hoped that he would be forgiven for the children's sake. "There will be," he said aloud, "still another chapter; perhaps several." He would wait and see.

Weeks and months passed. His madonna-wife made no sign of relenting, but she commenced no legal proceedings. The failure was not as bad as he had expected. Failures on Wall Street are queer affairs. Friendly brokers rally and help the insolvents into a few " good things;" in a year or so the failure is forgotten, and the firm is on a better basis than before. So it was with Beach, Catherly & De Ford. It came up again smiling. It was known that De Ford had had some trouble at home. But a man's private character or private family affairs are rarely inquired into minutely on 'Change. His friends stood by him. He was fortunate again and grew rich; so quickly do these ups and downs occur, where "business" is gambling on a large scale.

He did not break at once with Louise Franscioli. But he saw her, afterward, never alone. She seemed very much changed. One evening, after an absence of four days, he called at her apartment. She was gone. She had taken the Wednesday's French steamer, and French leave, the day before. She left him a sad, passionate little note, blotted with tears. In it she said, " If I go away forever, she will take you back."

It was noticed at the club that Challinor had suddenly sailed for Europe also. But Challinor was a man who did things largely from impulse, and he had the habit of going away suddenly to the ends of the earth at a moment's notice. Later on in the winter, his yacht, *Calypso,* received orders to sail for the Mediterranean.

De Ford, after that, became very cold and hard and indifferent to everything except business. His pride would never permit his making overtures of reconciliation to his wife, and his pride led him to the ambition of bequeathing an enormous fortune to his two children. To this, as the second year of their separation began, he consecrated himself with the devotion of an anchorite.

And what, then, is the end of this family history? After a third year of separation, did kindly intervening friends persuade the young wife and husband to forgive and forget? Did little Dorothy, as so often occurs in the play, lead "papa" to "mamma," and gently place "mamma's" hand in his for reconciliation? Or was a divorce obtained, and did Jack marry again, and, Mrs. Sundown dying, did Florence tearfully yield to the artist at last?

In real life, dear reader, these definite if not entirely satisfactory conclusions do not generally happen. In real life, longer periods of time seem to elapse before anything is decided. The fact is, that we would have to pry into the future to learn the final *denouement* of this little domestic tale. At present Florence is living very quietly with the two children, Dorothy and Jack, Jr., with the old folks in Gramercy Park. She does not go out at all, but is entirely absorbed in her children. Jack, Sr., never visits the old house on the Park, but the nurse takes the children to see him in his bachelor quarters on upper Broadway every Sunday afternoon. They are pretty, charming little things, and they ask poor Jack many awkward questions.

The blow of his disgrace was so shocking to Florence that it very nearly shattered her life. She was ill at the house of her friend, Mrs. Mitchell, a long time; but she recovered, and as the time went on she found consolation in religion and in charitable work, as well as in her children.

Once or twice, husband and wife have met by accident in street-cars or in public places. Mrs. Heath, who accompanied her daughter, has always spoken to Jack at these times. Once they met face to face at the dog-show. Mrs. Heath burst into tears, and pressed Jack's hand very kindly. There was never any doubt in his mind but that his dear old mother-in-law had long since forgiven him and that the reconciliation, if it comes, will come through the mediation of this sweet old lady. *She* was not a product of New England! Florence, at the times of these accidental encounters, avoided his glance and turned away. She has something of her father's Puritan nature. He, stern old New Englander, never was so contented in his home-life before. There is no one now to say him nay. He tyrannizes a little over his household, and directs a good deal in regard to the early religious training of Dorothy and Jack—whose name, by the way, he is exceedingly desirous of changing to Samuel—after himself. It is rather a pleasant sign, however, that Florence herself decidedly refuses to permit this. It is curious sometimes to see this sweet-faced mother lavish the most tender caresses on the sturdy youngster, her favorite, calling him again and again by name, and crying over him too, when she thinks no one is observing her.

As for De Ford, it may be said that he has once for all sown his wild-oats. He lives very quietly now at his club, dines out a good deal with his intimates. He is very reserved—and rather silent. He has made, and is making, a great deal of money. He talks seriously of going to Denver or San Francisco to live, is very silent concerning his personal affairs, and is regarded as a rising business man. He isn't forty yet, and doesn't drink. Ah well, there are some hopes for him!

"*And further this deponent saith not.*"

END.

D. APPLETON & CO.'S PUBLICATIONS.

APPLETONS' SUMMER SERIES, 1891.

TOURMALIN'S TIME CHEQUES. By F. ANSTEY, author of "Vice Versâ," "The Giant's Robe," etc.

"Its author has struck another rich vein of whimsicality and humor."—*San Francisco Argonaut.*

"His special gift is in making the impossible appear probable."—*St. Louis Republic.*

"A curious conceit and very entertaining story."—*Boston Advertiser.*

"Each cheque is good for several laughs."—*New York Herald.*

"Certainly one of the most diverting books of the season."—*Brooklyn Times.*

"Sets a handsome example for the 'Summer Series,' with its neat and portable style of half cloth binding and good paper and typography."—*Brooklyn Eagle.*

FROM SHADOW TO SUNLIGHT. By the MARQUIS OF LORNE.

"In these days of princely criticism—that is to say, criticism of princes—it is refreshing to meet a really good bit of aristocratic literary work, albeit the author is only a prince-in-law. . . . The theme chosen by the Marquis makes his story attractive to Americans."—*Chicago Tribune.*

"A charming book."—*Cincinnati Enquirer.*

ADOPTING AN ABANDONED FARM. By KATE SANBORN.

"It may be mythical, but it reads like a true narrative taken from a strong memory that has been re-enforced by a diary and corrected by the parish register. It is not only as natural as life, but, as Josh Billings used to say, 'even more so.'"—*New York Journal of Commerce.*

"A sunny, pungent, humorous sketch. . . . A bright, amusing book, which is thoughtful as well as amusing, and may stimulate, somewhere, thinking that shall bear fruit in some really effective remedial action."—*Chicago Times.*

ON THE LAKE OF LUCERNE, AND OTHER STORIES. By BEATRICE WHITBY.

"Six short stories carefully and conscientiously finished, and told with the graceful ease of the practiced *raconteur.*"—*Literary Digest.*

"The stories are pleasantly told in light and delicate vein, and are sure to be acceptable to the friends Miss Whitby has already made on this side of the Atlantic."—*Philadelphia Bulletin.*

"Very dainty, not only in mechanical workmanship but in matter and manner."—*Boston Advertiser.*

Each, 16mo, half cloth, with specially designed cover, 50 cents.

New York: D. APPLETON & CO., 1, 3, & 5 Bond Street.

ON THE PLANTATION. By JOEL CHANDLER HARRIS, author of "Uncle Remus." With 23 Illustrations by E. W. KEMBLE, and Portrait of the Author. 12mo. Cloth, $1.50.

"The book is in the characteristic vein which has made the author so famous and popular as an interpreter of plantation character."—*Rochester Union and Advertiser.*

"Those who never tire of Uncle Remus and his stories—with whom we would be accounted—will delight in Joe Maxwell and his exploits."—*London Saturday Review.*

"Altogether a most charming book."—*Chicago Times.*

"Really a valuable, if modest, contribution to the history of the civil war within the Confederate lines, particularly on the eve of the catastrophe. Two or three new animal fables are introduced with effect; but the history of the plantation, the printing-office, the black runaways, and white deserters, of whom the impending break-up made the community tolerant, the coon and fox hunting, forms the serious purpose of the book, and holds the reader's interest from beginning to end."—*New York Evening Post.*

UNCLE REMUS: *His Songs and his Sayings.* The Folk-lore of the Old Plantation. By JOEL CHANDLER HARRIS. Illustrated from Drawings by F. S. CHURCH and J. H. MOSER, of Georgia. 12mo. Cloth, $1.50.

"The idea of preserving and publishing these legends, in the form in which the old plantation negroes actually tell them, is altogether one of the happiest literary conceptions of the day. And very admirably is the work done. . . . In such touches lies the charm of this fascinating little volume of legends, which deserves to be placed on a level with *Reincke Fuchs* for its quaint humor, without reference to the ethnological interest possessed by these stories, as indicating, perhaps, a common origin for very widely severed races."—*London Spectator.*

"We are just discovering what admirable literary material there is at home, what a great mine there is to explore, and how quaint and peculiar is the material which can be dug up. Mr. Harris's book may be looked on in a double light—either as a pleasant volume recounting the stories told by a typical old colored man to a child, or as a valuable contribution to our somewhat meager folk-lore. . . . To Northern readers the story of Brer (Brother—Brudder) Rabbit may be novel. To those familiar with plantation life, who have listened to these quaint old stories, who have still tender reminiscences of some good old mauma who told these wondrous adventures to them when they were children, Brer Rabbit, the Tar Baby, and Brer Fox come back again with all the past pleasures of younger days."—*New York Times.*

"Uncle Remus's sayings on current happenings are very shrewd and bright, and the plantation and revival songs are choice specimens of their sort."—*Boston Journal.*

New York: D. APPLETON & CO., 1, 3, & 5 Bond Street.

www.ingramcontent.com/pod-product-compliance
Lightning Source LLC
Chambersburg PA
CBHW021842230426
43669CB00008B/1048